understanding judith Butler

understanding judith Butler
anita brady and tony schirato

Los Angeles | London | New Delhi
Singapore | Washington DC

SAGE Publications Ltd
1 Oliver's Yard
55 City Road
London EC1Y 1SP

SAGE Publications Inc.
2455 Teller Road
Thousand Oaks, California 91320

SAGE Publications India Pvt Ltd
B 1/I 1 Mohan Cooperative Industrial Area
Mathura Road
New Delhi 110 044

SAGE Publications Asia-Pacific Pte Ltd
33 Pekin Street #02-01
Far East Square
Singapore 048763

Library of Congress Control Number: 2010925733

British Library Cataloguing in Publication data

A catalogue record for this book is available from the British Library

ISBN 978-1-84787-607-2
ISBN 978-1-84787-608-9 (pbk)

Typeset by C&M Digitals (P) Ltd, Chennai, India
Printed by CPI Antony Rowe, Chippenham, Wiltshire
Printed on paper from sustainable resources

MIX
Paper from
responsible sources
FSC
www.fsc.org   FSC® C013604

Contents

Introduction

I would like to start, and to end, with the question of the human, of who counts
as human, and the related question of whose lives count as lives, and with a question that has preoccupied many of us for years: what makes for a grievable life?
(Butler 2004: 17–18)

In the range of critiques that followed the publication of Judith Butler's
Gender Trouble: Feminism and the Subversion of Identity (1990), among
the most persistent were those that contended that this text – with its dense
and complex language, its commitment to the possibilities of parody and
trouble, and its central contention that both the category of women, and the
bodies that mark one as belonging to that category, are constructions – was
at a significant, and possibly dangerous, remove from the real lives of the real
bodies of the real women with which feminist theory should be concerned.
Yet the critical consideration that *Understanding Butler* undertakes demonstrates a persistent impetus across Butler's body of work that is at odds with
the logic of such critiques, and is much more in keeping with the quotation
from *Undoing Gender* above. At the centre of her work is the seemingly
simple question of which bodies get to count as human – which bodies get to
matter, get to be considered worth protecting, are worth grieving for – and
which bodies do not, and are condemned, instead, to what Butler refers to as
an unlivable life. This book asserts that this question of which bodies count
as human is a question that has preoccupied Butler 'for years'.

Like Butler, we 'would like to start, and to end, with the question of the
human' (2004: 17). Rather than a chronological account of Butler's work,
this book is instead organised around the five central areas of study – what
we might call themes or problematics – with which her work is concerned:
subjectivity, gender, queer, symbolic violence and ethics. In a sense, these
themes can be described as trajectories of the human: the conditions under
which it is brought into existence; the specifics under which it is categorised

and simultaneously constituted; the ways in which that constitution might be undone, or, at the very least, troubled by the contradictions that characterise the management of desire; the violence that seems to persist in the relations between humans, and that is found to be integral to the very terms by which those subjects are brought into being; and finally the ethics attendant upon the subject that finds itself cognisant of the conditions under which it is made – conditions and mechanisms of power that both enable it to know of the impossibility of being able to speak of itself, or for the other, but that simultaneously impose upon it a responsibility to do so.

In order to understand Butler's work, it is imperative to consider the theoretical and philosophical contexts within which that work emerges, and with which she is always engaged. The theoretical resources on which Butler draws are considerable and daunting in their scope, but of particular importance (and thus given particular attention here) is the work of Foucault, Hegel, Nietzsche, Bourdieu, Freud, Lacan and the fields of feminist and queer theory. Each chapter contextualises her work in relation to the relevant thinkers on which it draws, and utilises examples and events to elucidate the theoretical models she proposes, and to demonstrate the ongoing importance of her work.

Understanding Butler takes the following form. Chapter 1, 'Subjectivity, Identity and Desire', examines Butler's account of the formation of the body as a culturally intelligible site that comes to have the status of subject. It draws in particular on *Subjects of Desire* (1987) and *The Psychic Life of Power* (1997b), and on the work of Hegel, Freud, Lacan and Foucault. The chapter considers the relationship between subjectivity and desire; the distinctions Butler makes between subjectivity and identity; and the mechanism of subjection, whereby the subject is dependent for its existence upon the very regimes of power that constrain the possible forms that its existence *as* a subject might take.

In Chapter 2, 'Gender', we look in detail at the specific subjectivating mechanism with which Butler is most concerned – the system of gender. *Gender Trouble* (1990) is, by far, Butler's best known work, a fact not altogether unsurprising when one considers that Butler's project within it is to query the very subject of feminism – the category 'women'. Butler argues that feminism's uncritical commitment to this category risks reifying the very systems of gender oppression that feminism seeks to oppose. In this chapter we examine both the terms and the significance of Butler's intervention through a consideration of her critique of the category women, and her critique of the distinction between sex and gender that, at the time *Gender Trouble* was written, dominated feminist theory. For Butler, both sex *and* gender are discursive constructions, and in this chapter we consider why Butler contends that both can only 'materialise' through what she terms the 'heterosexual matrix' of intelligibility. If *Gender Trouble* is her best known work, then the model of performativity that it offers as a means of both understanding how sex and gender are constituted within that matrix, and as a possible mechanism for disturbing that constitution, is perhaps her most significant theoretical contribution, and Chapter 2 concludes with a consideration of how the notion of 'gender performativity' works.

The model of performativity that Butler develops in *Gender Trouble* and *Bodies That Matter* (1993), and the possibilities it offers for the subversion of gender norms, are integral to the field of queer theory. Chapter 3, 'Queer', examines the significance of Butler's critique of identity for the theoretical and political deployment of the notion of 'queer'. It begins by situating Butler's theorising of the relationship between sexual identity and heteronormativity within the context of a lesbian and gay politics dominated by a commitment to identity. It then considers the significance of Butler's work to the field of queer theory, and the often complex relationship between that field, and the field of feminist theory from which *Gender Trouble* emerged. Of particular concern to Butler is the tendency within queer theory to assign the study of gender to feminism, and the study of sexuality to the realm of queer. Butler insists, instead, that sex, gender and sexuality are indissociable from the heteronormative matrix within which all subjects acquire recognition.

Issues of recognition, and of the violence that necessarily accompanies both its operation and its absence, are the subjects of Chapter 4, 'Symbolic Violence'. This chapter examines the ways in which the lines of the recognisably human are demarcated and sustained through symbolic violence. Rather than simply tracking the recognisably violent acts that are routinely deployed to police the edges of subjectivity (gay-bashing might be such an example), Butler looks instead at how the demarcations of what gets to count as violence effect their own violence, even as such demarcations fail to acknowledge precisely how and where violence is done. To put this more simply: to insult a boy by calling him a girl may do violence to that boy as an everyday mechanism of shaming him in highly gendered terms, yet its distinction as violence (whether to him or to the girls it wields as an insult) may simultaneously cover over the extent to which violence is done to the boy by calling him a *boy*. For Butler, symbolic violence is integral to the operation of power, and inextricably bound up with the discursive authority to confer recognition. This chapter draws on *Excitable Speech* (1997a), *Precarious Life* (2006) and *Antigone's Claim* (2000), in particular, to work through Butler's consideration of the relationship between symbolic violence and what constitutes the livable, and the grievable, life. To that end, this chapter considers the discursive politics of hatespeech, and the post-9/11 context of a global 'war on terror'.

In our final chapter, 'Ethics', we consider how Butler theorises and analyses those situations where the silence that accompanies the normal, natural and doxic gives way to an anxiety and concomitant speech that is trying, in Foucaltian terms, to 'take care of something' – whether it be the notion of truth, the parameters of socio-cultural duty, or more generally the various accounts cultures give of themselves. The chapter largely focuses on *Giving an Account of Oneself* (2005) and *Precarious Life*, and deals with Butler's accounts of the work of Foucault and Levinas. To quote from Foucault, we can say that much of Butler's later work focuses on 'the events that have led us to constitute ourselves and to recognize ourselves as subjects of what we are doing, thinking, saying' (Foucault 1997: 315).

1 Subjectivity, identity and desire

INTRODUCTION

'The question of "the subject"', Butler writes in the first chapter of *Gender Trouble*, 'is crucial for politics' (1990: 2). The explicit departure point for Butler's interrogation of the relation between subjectivity and identity is the discussion, in that text, of the extent to which there is a universal basis for feminist politics. Specifically, the issue she addresses is whether or not the presumption of a series of identities or categories (women, feminism, masculinity, patriarchy, the West), consistent and continuous across historical periods and various cultural sites and contexts, can be justified. Her point is that any feminist political project cannot simply presume or take for granted the terms through which it acts, since such terms (and the meanings associated with them) are the product of the discursive regime and field of power that feminism wishes to challenge. Moreover, there is no point in simply appealing to or working through institutions of authority such as the law, if the field of law is one of the key sites for producing and naturalising the conditions of gender hegemony and violence. In other words, for Butler the politics of identity is always derived from, dependent on, and only explicable in terms of, a prior politics of subjectivity.

THE SUBJECT OF THE BODY

The set of issues Butler takes up in *Subjects of Desire* (1987) and *Gender Trouble*, and then follows and develops throughout her oeuvre (but most particularly in *Bodies That Matter* (1993) and *The Psychic Life of Power* (1997b)) is derived from Foucault's observation that 'juridical systems of power produce the subjects they subsequently come to represent' (Butler

1990: 2). This means that all forms of identity and identification (including those pertaining to gender) are based on and linked to the procedures, processes, techniques and structures of subjectivity, or what Butler in *The Psychic Life of Power* refers to as the process of subjection. Therefore in order to have, gain, claim or be assigned an identity, one must be recognisable and explicable within a particular grid of intelligibility that makes subjects appear, and authorises the subject's status as an identity-in-waiting:

> Juridical subjects are invariably produced through certain exclusionary practices that do not 'show' once the juridical structure of politics has been established ... the political construction of the subject proceeds with certain legitimating and exclusionary aims, and these political operations are effectively concealed and naturalized ... Juridical power inevitably 'produces' what it claims merely to represent ... It is not enough to inquire into how women might become more fully represented in language and politics. Feminist critique ought also to understand how the category of 'women' ... is produced and restrained by the very structures of power through which emancipation is sought. (Butler 1990: 2)

Butler's discussion of the 'Joan/John' case, in *Undoing Gender* (2004), demonstrates how bodies are constituted as recognisable subjects, or otherwise. The case concerns the situation of David Reimer, who was born with XY chromosomes but at an early age had his penis severed in a botched medical operation. After consulting Dr John Money of the Gender Identity Institute, Reimer's parents accepted the strong recommendation that he be raised as a girl. His testicles were surgically removed, and plans made to create a vagina. At the age of nine, however, the renamed 'Brenda' started to behave in a manner and develop preferences (regarding toys, desires, toilet etiquette, etc.) that marked her as different from other girls. This was followed by various attempted medical interventions – all strongly resisted by her – that sought, amongst other things, to dispose and help facilitate Brenda to 'become a girl', in both a medical and a socio-cultural sense:

> At this point, the psychiatric teams that were intermittently monitoring Brenda's adaptation offered her estrogen, and she refused this. Money tried to talk to her about getting a real vagina, and she refused; in fact, she went screaming from the room. Money had her view sexually graphic pictures of vaginas. Money even went so far as to show Brenda pictures of women giving birth, holding out the promise that Brenda might be able to give birth if she acquired a vagina ... she and her brother were required to perform mock coital exercises with one another, on command. They both later reported being very frightened and disoriented. (2004: 60)

Money claimed, clearly contrary to the experience of Brenda, that the intervention was both a success and a demonstration that 'the gender identity gate is open at birth for a normal child no less than for one born with unfinished sex organs' (p. 61). His critics read his actions as ideologically driven and evidence that biology was 'sufficient grounds for the presumption of social masculinity' (p. 63). Butler, on the other hand, is more concerned with showing the:

> Disciplinary framework within which Brenda/David develops a discourse of self-reporting and self-understanding, since it constitutes the grid of intelligibility by which his own humanness is both questioned and asserted ... There was an apparatus of knowledge applied to the person and body ... Brenda was subjected to such scrutiny and, most importantly, constantly and repeatedly subjected to a norm, a normalizing ideal that was conveyed through a plurality of gazes, a norm applied to the body ... these exercises interrogate whether the gender norm that establishes a coherent personhood has been successfully accomplished. The inquiries and inspections can be understood ... as the violent attempt to implement the norm, and the institutionalization of that power of implementation. (pp. 67–8)

If the context and background of sexual and gender identity, for instance, is the presumption and naturalisation of heteronormativity, then the human body becomes explicable within processes of discursive designation and location: the body-as-content is designated as being commensurate, or otherwise, with regard to socio-cultural and/or scientific categories, and is thus inscribed in terms of certain meanings, values, dispositions, orientations and narratives. This is why the case of Brenda/David is scandalous: it denies any obvious consistent or necessary articulation between and across the body, sex and sexuality.

Butler takes up the question of the relation between subjectivity, identity, normalisation and the materiality of the body more fully in *Bodies That Matter* (1993). That book is usually read in terms of Butler's reworking of the notion of gender performativity, a reading partly attributable to criticism that such a notion effectively reduced gender to at best unmediated agency, and at worst a form of fashion. Analysis of this criticism is dealt with elsewhere in this book; what is pertinent here is how *Bodies That Matter* addresses the intractable nature of the body, and how that body plays out within the context of the constitutive powers and work performed by normative discourses. Butler is particularly interested in the status of corporeality. What does it mean, for instance, to say that the body is 'constructed' through norms? Or again, what response can be provided in the face of the 'truth' of bodily presence, the self-evidence of materiality, the obviousness of the assertion, made while vigorously patting or prodding oneself, that 'my stomach exists'? Butler turns this position on its head by asking how we can possibly come to treat the act of construction, which makes the body intelligible, and organises and enables us to see it, as something 'artificial and dispensable' (1993: xi).

Something seemingly as obvious, unmediated and commonsensical as the parts of the body – the stomach, arms, feet, neck, genitals, etc. – are only visible and distinctive in terms of their relation to, and differentiation from, other parts of the overall structure. So for instance in everyday popular (rather than physiological) understanding, the stomach begins somewhere below the chest and ends above the groin and the genitals, and reaches its limits on either side at the hips (below) and the ribs (above); while there is that disconcertingly anonymous area in between that attracts the designation in the absence of a designation, called 'the side'. At the level of the physiological sciences, while the categories, points of differentiation and specific characteristics that correspond with or constitute the parts of the body are more definite, the charts that neatly plot and represent the parameters and locations of organs, muscles, ligaments, blood vessels and bones disguise the reality that spaces are blurred or shared, categories overlap, and imbrication, rather than separation, is the reality.

When considering how the parts of the body are seen, we have to remember that the various systems of categorisation, explication and representation – the commonsensical everyday, the scientific, the quasi-scientific, the religious, the culinary, and those that are associated with and implicit in popular culture genres such as romance, pornography and sport, to name but a few – are at best connected to and translatable into one another by way of a vague family resemblance, rather than rigorous scientific equation or correspondence. Moreover, this lack of correspondence across systems of categorisation is even more pronounced when we take into account historical and technological differences. The scientific body clearly feeds into and influences the popular version of the body, but in periods prior to the emergence of science (or for that matter, writing) the body, at the level of the commonsensical and everyday, was categorised, organised and recognised in ways that would have been unthinkable to the contemporary world. We only have to consider Foucault's well-known citation from Borges's fiction regarding:

> a 'certain Chinese encyclopaedia' in which it is written that 'animals' are divided into: (a) belonging to the emperor, (b) embalmed, (c) tame, (d) sucking pigs, (e) sirens, (f) fabulous, (g) stray dogs, (h) included in the present classification, (i) frenzied, (j) innumerable, (k) drawn with a very fine camelhair brush, (l) et cetera, (m) having just broken the water pitcher, (n) that from a long way off look like flies. (1973: xv)

As Foucault writes, 'In the wonderment of this taxonomy ... the thing that ... is demonstrated', along with the 'exotic charm of another system of thought', is precisely 'the limitation of our own, the stark impossibility of thinking that' (p. xv).

The point he is making here is that systems of categorisation don't just arrange content: they both naturalise a certain mediated version of the world, and simultaneously render anything else more or less unthinkable. So when Butler refers to the contemporary body being constructed via regulatory systems and forms of normativity, she is referring to the twin operations of production and foreclosure, whereby 'bodies only appear, only endure, only live within the productive constraints of certain highly gendered regulatory schemas' (1993: xi).

NARRATIVES OF THE BODY

The notion that the construction of the body involves significant variations in systems of categorisation is further complicated because different contexts – historical, cultural, national, religious, economic, political and generic – determine or inflect the way the body is understood, the meanings that are associated with it, and the narratives and values that come to inhabit it. Every cultural field, for instance, not only determines what kinds of bodies are cognate with regard to its particular ethos, values and logics – it also ascribes cultural capital to certain types of bodies and denies it to others. This involves prescribing the forms of bodily hexis (movements, deportment, production of points of focus or emphasis) that are commensurate with, and appropriately represent, the values of a cultural field; and providing each and every body with a narrative (regarding the necessity of transforming the body, the body becoming aesthetic project, the body being denied, etc.). In some fields (religion, science, the law) the body has a limited, technical or even undesirable status, while in others (sport, advertising, fashion) it is the centre of attention, and largely stands in for, or does the discursive work of, the field.

The same sorts of differences are played out at the level of popular cultural genre. In romance novels and films, for instance, the body has an ambivalent status. To some extent it is something that has to be denied or at least underplayed: given that the *raison d'être* of popular romantic love is the surpassing of the body, the identification of something (a value, an essence, an affinity) that is 'more than this' (love will endure, it will outlast the corporeal), then the body, from this perspective, is the site of false love (temporary physical attraction, lust). If love is eternal and the body is ephemeral, then romantic love cannot be embodied. However given that most popular romance genres and narratives emphasise, or even require, a classically attractive, youthful, or sexually desirable or available body, then some narrative sleight-of-hand is required to ensure that the body matters, without appearing to replace the primacy of the spirit or the soul. The way this is usually done, for instance in contemporary teen films or Disney youth television shows, is to project a correspondence (or otherwise) between physical and spiritual beauty or value; in other words, the real heroine will be attractive, but also good, kind, selfless, caring and loyal, while the false heroine will be attractive in a way that draws attention to her personality failings as a romantic heroine (she will be vain, spend too much time on clothes or make-up). Effectively the real heroine is a beautiful body that denies or downplays – and thus surpasses – the body, while the false heroine is only a body. This, in perhaps the most instantly recognisable example of this point, Snow White, when she is not cooking for the Seven Dwarves, is immobilised and effectively 'out of body', while the Evil Queen is obsessed with her image in the mirror.

Butler asks us to think about which bodies can appear and endure 'within the productive constraints of ... regulatory schemas' (1993: xi). Another, perhaps more specific, way of looking at this issue is to consider the extent to which certain types of bodies fit in with, or correspond to, the norms associated with different socio-cultural narratives, genres and cultural fields. It is not simply a case of whether or not bodies are explicable or otherwise; regulation of the body is also concerned with regimes of value which organise, deploy and arrange bodies within and across spaces, and which facilitate or deny – and naturalise – certain trajectories. Regulation of the body, from this perspective, is both an act of construction (bodies are brought into being via a grid of intelligibility) and a form of architecture (they are set in motion and disposed in accordance with the arrangement of socio-cultural sites and spaces). Within different cultural fields, for instance, the body is only 'allowed to endure' to the extent to which it embodies, and performs in accordance with, a specific ethos. As Bourdieu makes clear with regard to the scientific field, to be admitted does not simply entail satisfying objective criteria and displaying technical competence (in terms of educational qualifications and methodological literacies, say); rather, the scientific habitus must be embodied in a consistent and convincing manner (2004: 51). The conditions within each field generally reflect or perhaps refract regimes of value and narratives characteristic of the wider social field: so the disinterested, rational and serious body of science is also predominantly a male body, even when the scientist is female. As Evelyn Fox Keller points out in her study of the gendering of science, what is at issue is not simply:

> the relative absence of women in science. Although it is true that most scientists have been ... men, the makeup of the scientific population hardly counts, by itself, for the attribution of masculinity to science as an intellectual domain ... To both scientists and their public, scientific thought is male thought ... as Simmel observed, objectivity itself is an ideal that has a long history of identification with masculinity ... A woman thinking scientifically or objectively is thinking 'like a man'. (1985: 76–7)

Much the same kind of specific logic applies in popular culture genres and their narratives. We pointed out that in romance the body is both crucial and irrelevant: what is usually put into play is a conventionally attractive and sexually desirable (which normally means young) body which must be shown to be extraneous to what is at stake (romantic love), or a reflection of inner virtues (a tendency to smile reveals a pleasant nature, a healthy body demonstrates restraint and responsibility). What is clear, however, is that despite its apparent irrelevance, body typologies have a narrative dimension. Although a classically attractive body is not necessarily synonymous with authentic romantic feeling, having a classically unattractive body certainly directs characters away from the position of romantic 'seriousness'. The older, or awkward, or non-honed body can, in popular culture texts, be in love and be loved in return, and experience genuine romance, but usually at a secondary level – as a comic refraction of, or a narrative supplement to, the main romance. In other words, while the non-romantic body can experience romance, this is rarely put forward as an exemplary or normal situation; rather it is the exception that proves the rule, and it is precisely in the insistence that the exception can happen (the geek or the so-called overweight character finds love despite their physicality) that we come to recognise that it isn't the norm.

BODIES, SUBJECTS AND IDENTITIES

The work of normalisation, then, is carried out by way of the repeated representation and deployment, in popular culture texts and discourses, of bodies that are rendered explicable in terms of certain regimes of value (they are sexually attractive; they incite desire, envy, admiration and identification) and narratives (they are naturally disposed to achieve popularity, happiness, success). Put simply, the norm is what makes each and every body meaningful, and by extension recognisable (or otherwise). This is what Butler is referring to when she proposes, in *Bodies That Matter*:

> a return to the notion of matter, not as site or surface, but as a process of materialization that stabilizes over time to produce the effects of boundary, fixity, and surface we call matter. That matter is always materialized has, I think, to be thought in relation to the productive and, indeed materializing effects of regulatory power in the Foucaltian sense. (1993: 10–11)

There are five closely connected aspects to this 'reformulation of the materiality of bodies' (1993: 2). First, in much the same way that Nietzsche (1956) could claim that meaning is a manifestation of power, Butler proposes that the body must be understood as 'the effect of a dynamic of power' (1993: 2). Second, the reiteration of discourses, performances and narratives of – and the repeated confirmation of relations of value regarding – the body, and their strategic deployment across social and cultural fields, effectively work to make bodies potentially visible and recognisable as coherent sets of forms, categories and meanings. Third, this recognition of the body is the first step in an ongoing process that leads to the production of a subject, and the discursive practices of identification. Fourth, the association of bodily exemplars and typologies with authorised meanings, narratives and values functions as a norm, in the Foucaltian sense; that is, it disciplines, disposes and orients subjects. Fifth, Butler points out that this process by which subjects are formed and disposed is dependent not just on what is allowed, but also on what is denied. Referring to the quite vexed and complex linkage between subjectivity and identification, she suggests that, with regard to the movement from sex to sexuality:

> The heterosexual imperative enables certain sexed identifications and forecloses and/or disavows other identifications. This exclusionary matrix by which subjects are formed thus requires the simultaneous production of a domain of abject beings, those who are not yet 'subjects', but who form the constitutive outside to the domain of the subject. The abject designates here precisely those 'unlivable' and 'uninhabitable' zones of social life which are nevertheless densely populated by those who do not enjoy the status of the subject, but whose living under the sign of the 'unlivable' is required to circumscribe the domain of the subject. This zone of uninhabitability ... will constitute that site of dreaded identification against which ... the domain of the subject will circumscribe its own claim to autonomy and to life. In this sense, then, the subject is constituted through the force of exclusion and abjection, one which ... is, after all, 'inside' the subject as its own founding repudiation. (1993: 3)

This articulation of the process whereby a body eventually assumes the status of subject and takes on various identities is straightforward enough – up to a point. The problem occurs when we try to make sense of the relation between subjectivity and identity. Butler is not particularly helpful or clear on this issue. In the paragraph from which we have just quoted from *Bodies That Matter*, she is at pains to point out that a subject does not assume a bodily norm (that is, is assigned a sex), but rather the reverse – it is the process of assuming a sex that brings the subject into being (1993: 3). She then links this process with 'the question of identification, and with the discursive means by which the heterosexual imperative enables certain sexed identifications and forecloses ... other identifications' (p. 3). The term 'identification' has an interesting status here. It seems to be understood, firstly, as something that takes place subsequent to becoming a subject (and being assigned a sex), and secondly, as connoting a form of agency. So I am categorised as male or female, and then certain choices are apparently available to me: my desire can be turned in the direction of the opposite sex (which is not just available, but also authorised, expected and designated as normal); or I can take the option which is no option at all, the option which is foreclosed, and turn my desire in the direction of the same sex as myself.

A number of questions need to be raised apropos of this issue. What is involved in identification? Does it refer, for instance, to a practice where the subject exercises some form of agency and effectively chooses one option over another? To what extent can we make space for this notion of identification-as-agency when Butler quite clearly insists, following Foucault, that power is always prior to and constitutive of the body-as-subject; in other words, where does identification come from, how is it produced and disposed, and what accounts for its misfirings and misperformances? To a certain extent any attempt to address these questions requires the posing of another even more complex set of questions, concerning the relation between, and the differentiation of, the concepts of the subject (and subjectivity) and identification and, most crucially, how this relation is informed by the notion of desire.

SUBJECTS OF DESIRE

Subjects of Desire (1987) and *The Psychic Life of Power* (1997b) constitute two very different attempts to deal with these issues. The former is sub-titled 'Hegelian Reflections in Twentieth Century France', and Butler writes that the main task of this book is to:

> comprehend retrospectively ... the formulation of desire and satisfaction in Hegel's Phenomenology of Spirit, its philosophical celebration and reconstruction by some twentieth-century French philosophers, and the incipient moment of Hegel's dissolution in France through the deployment of desire to refute Hegel's metaphysically supported subject. (1987: 7)

Hegel formulates desire as the vehicle that effectively produces consciousness and the subject, but as Butler asks, what kind of vehicle is it (p. ix)? Desire in Hegel is understood as or stands in for reflexive consciousness, whereby consciousness seeks to know and comprehend itself through the mediation of otherness. This is how, for Hegel, the reflexive subject is formed: desire moves consciousness outside of itself to form a relation with the world-as-difference, which in turn reflects and demonstrates both the limits of the subject (I can only know myself through reference to the process of mediation and connectedness with the other), and its conditions of being (I continue to exist and know myself by way of my relation to difference). Butler's metaphor of desire-as-vehicle is particularly apt here; the Hegelian subject 'expands in the course of its adventure through alterity; it internalises the world it desires, and expands to encompass, to be, what it initially confronts as other to itself' (p. 9). The desire of desire is, for Hegel, the subject's (continual) discovery of itself in the world, understood as a form of knowledge (pp. 24–5).

Much of *Subjects of Desire* is taken up with Hegel's reception in France, initially through Marxism (particularly Alexander Kojeve) and phenomenology (Sartre); and then in what she refers to as 'contemporary French thought', encompassing psychoanalysis (Lacan) and what has been described (see Best and Kellner 1991) as postmodern theory (Foucault, Deleuze). Kojeve's appropriation of Hegel's conceptualisation of desire is more of an extension than a development or critique: briefly however, we can say that one of his more important contributions to the theory of desire is the distinction he makes between ordinary biological (animal) and human desire. Human desire, for Kojeve, is precisely the overcoming and transcending of biological desire and nature – it comes before and constitutes the subject. In other words, while the order of nature has no way of seeing the world except in terms of biological needs, human desire 'exhibits a structure of reflexivity ... Kojeve's subject is an essentially intentional structure' (p. 67).

Hegelian and post-Hegelian (Kojeve, Hypolite, Sartre) accounts of the role played by desire in the constitution of the subject emphasise its productive dimension, specifically the work it does to overcome the negativity that characterises human life. This negativity (that is, the purely biological, the animal, base identity) is effectively negated and transformed by the subject-becoming-human, which involves a thinking on and producing narratives of (and connections with) the world. Desire, from this perspective, instigates and facilitates the work of creating 'a metaphysically pleasurable fictive world, fully present and devoid of negativity' (p. 185). Even in Sartre's critique of Hegel, where instead of self-recovery the subject 'is projected endlessly, without recovery' (p. 185), it nevertheless remains 'a fictive unity projected in words' that 'knows itself in its estrangement and so remains a unitary consciousness' (p. 185). This situation changes, in France, when Hegelian thought is subjected to critiques from Lacanian psychoanalysis, and postmodern theory derived from or strongly influenced by Nietzsche. The subject is still 'understood as a projected unity, but this projection disguises and falsifies the multiplicitous disunity constitutive of experience, whether conceived as libidinal forces, the will-to-power, or the various strategies of power/discourse' (p. 185).

Lacanian psychoanalysis retains Hegel's notion of desire as having a structural role in the formation of the subject, but instead of simply serving the ends of consciousness, now desire and consciousness are connected by, and relate to one another in terms of, a necessary deception. Following Freud, Lacan posits desire as something that is sent away in order that the subject can exist; however repressed desire always returns without overtly manifesting or articulating itself, in dreams or other 'displacements, ruptures, and fissures of consciousness itself' (p. 186). For psychoanalytical theory, the notion of a reflexive, self-knowing subject is a myth: the subject is always constituted and characterised by forces that it not only cannot control, but which it cannot (and must not) know or acknowledge.

The status of desire is similarly differentiated from its place in the Hegelian narrative. Freud and Lacan understand desire as a form of libidinal energy; but whereas Freud tends to think of this energy in terms of specific unconscious wishes, Lacan opts for a less domesticated account of its workings. As Laplanche and Pontalis point out, he distinguishes desire from:

> concepts with which it is often confused, such as need and demand. Need is directed towards a specific object and is satisfied by it. Demands are formulated and addressed to others; where they are still aimed at an object, this is not essential to them, since the articulated demand is essentially a demand for love. Desire appears in the rift which separates need and demand; it cannot be reduced to need since ... it is not a relation to a real object independent of the subject but a relation to phantasy; nor can it be reduced to demand, in that it seeks to impose itself without taking the language or the unconscious of the other into account, and insists upon absolute recognition from him. (1988: 483)

Whereas Hegel understands desire as a form of mediation that produces self-knowledge, Lacan foregrounds what Butler refers to as the 'opacity of desire' (1987: 186): the Oedipus complex (which we deal with, in some detail, in Chapter 2) constitutes the subject by sending desire (for the mother) away, but this repression of desire produces the subject as lack and incomplete, and inaugurates a cycle of 'desiring for a desire' that would complete the subject. As Butler writes, 'The bar or prohibition that separates the subject from the unconscious is a negative relation which fails to mediate what it separates' (p. 187). Whereas Kojève could differentiate between biological and human forms of desire, and find in that difference the basis of a teleological narrative (progress, becoming human, rationality, knowledge, reflexivity),

Lacanian desire is unruly, undomesticated and defined by its own internal incoherence; it is split, like the subject it constitutes, between the satisfaction of biological needs and the demand for the other's love.

This idea of a split in desire is borrowed from Freud's notion of anaclisis, whereby the initial instinct of self-preservation (sucking the breast for nourishment) is used as a kind of prop by the sexual instincts. Jean Laplanche describes this 'propping of the drive on the function' as having two phases:

> In the first phase – breast-sucking for nourishment – we are faced with a function or ... totally instinctual pattern of behavior, which ... the 'popular conception' assumes to be the model of every instinct. It is an instinctual pattern with its impetus ... an accumulation of tensions; a 'source', as well, the digestive system ... A specific object ... not the breast ... but the nourishment: milk. Finally there is a performed process or 'aim', the process of breast sucking ... Now the crucial point is that simultaneous with the feeding function's achievement of satisfaction in nourishment, a sexual process begins to appear ... the mouth is simultaneously a sex organ and an organ of the feeding function. Thus the 'propping' consists initially in that support which emergent sexuality finds in the function linked to the preservation of life. (1990: 17)

Butler quotes Lacan to the effect that 'desire is neither the appetite for satisfaction, nor the demand for love, but the difference that results from the subtraction of the first from the second, the phenomenon of their splitting' (Lacan 1977: 287). The propping of the sexual instincts on the feeding function does not in any sense satisfy desire since, like the subject who arrives through and abides by way of a lack, the sexual instinct can only seek out substitutes for the mother's (or nurse's) breast, what Freud refers to as the process of anaclitic identification (Freud 1986). In psychoanalysis 'That which is thus alienated in needs ... reappears in man as desire ... The phenomenology that emerges is ... paradoxical, deviant, erratic, eccentric, even scandalous' (Lacan 1977: 286) in its differentiation from those instincts associated with self-preservation.

The last move Butler makes in her critique of Hegelian accounts and narratives of desire is made by way of reference to the strongly Nietzschean-influenced work of Deleuze and Foucault. Deleuze's main target is the notion that desire is tied to or predicated on negativity, something that is articulated not just in psychoanalytical theory (as the desire for a desire), but also in

Christian morality (desire must be defeated), and capitalist imperatives and discourses (you desire what you lack). As Butler points out, this doesn't mean that Deleuze denies the centrality of desire in human activity; on the contrary, and following Nietzsche, he insists 'there is only desire and the social, and nothing else' (Deleuze and Guattari 1989: 29). Desire for Nietzsche and Deleuze is the will manifested as the affirmation of life-as-force:

> The Nietzschean will is ... a multiplicitous play of forces which cannot be constrained by as dialectical unity; these forces represent currents of life, interests, desires, pleasures, and thoughts ... The Nietzschean will ... does not affirm itself apart from the context of alterity, but differs from Hegelian desire in its fundamental approach to alterity ... otherness no longer presents itself as that to be ... superseded or conceptualised; rather, difference is the condition for enjoyment, an enhanced sense of pleasure, the acceleration and intensification of the play of forces which constitute what we might call Nietzsche's version of jouissance ... Deleuze describes this difference between Nietzsche and Hegel: 'Nietzsche's "yes" is opposed to the dialectical "no"'. (Butler 1987: 208–9)

History, for Deleuze, can be understood as an account of will that has been gradually enslaved and turned against itself. An example is the Nietzschean narrative of how the Christian doctrine of forgiveness and self-abasement was promulgated by those who would exercise their will and dominate others; however because they were weak, they lacked the capacity to do so. Instead, they achieved their aim by subterfuge – the weak conspired to convince their opponents that strength was weakness, will arrogance, and desire a vice. This mindset produced a violence directed against the self.

Foucault offers an altogether different historical account of desire – a genealogy, in the Nietzschean sense of the term. Genealogy can be understood as an attempt to trace and locate the moments and sites when power produces and naturalises meaning or sense. Historical narratives and discourses, for instance, are produced to legitimate and authorise the claims or rights of one group at the expense of another, and to make it seem as if this is merely the way of the world, the way things are and were meant to be. The idea is that a particular substance or thing (a class faction, a race, a gender, an age group) is made to appear synonymous with an attribute (knowledge, civilisation, rationality). Nietzsche offers the example of the 'etymology of the terms for good in various languages', all of which taken together:

lead us back to the same conceptual transformation. The basic concept is always noble in the hierarchical, class sense, and from this has developed, by historical necessity, the concept of good embracing nobility of mind, spiritual distinction. This development is strictly parallel to that other which eventually converted the notions common, plebian, base into the notion bad. (1956: 162)

Genealogy is opposed, then, to official or traditional history that performs the work of naturalising power; and the work of history to which Foucault gives his attention is that of 'the cultural construction of desire' (Butler 1987: 215). The main difference between Foucault's approach and that of the Hegelian tradition (and even psychoanalysis) is that, for Foucault, desire is first and foremost a name with a history – in other words, its status is fundamentally discursive. More specifically, Foucault reverses the logic of Hegelian and psychoanalytic accounts of desire that situate it as prior to, and largely constitutive of, culture. We have seen that for Hegel desire facilitates reflexivity and mediates the world, bringing the subject into being. In Freud's work, the law barring incestuous desire is the path that both anchors the subject while splitting it by way of repression: as with the Hegelian tradition, the relationship between desire and sublimation is the mechanism, for Freud, by which civilisation supersedes the biological and instinctual. Similarly for Lacan, what Butler refers to as the 'juridical model of power' posits 'a true desire prior to repression, a phenomenon that would, according to Foucault, announce an "outside" to discourse' (1987: 221). Foucault, however, insists that the concept of desire is something that is only intelligible within, and produced by, discursive practices and formations; in other words, power precedes both desire and the subject.

Moreover there is a great deal at stake, for various formations of power, in being able to define, explain and deploy the concept of desire as a form of truth or an aspect of knowledge. As a privileged form of truth, desire authorises socio-cultural narratives and explanations; provides the basis for the categorisation of subjects and their bodies; and is identified as that which must be either embraced, affirmed, negated or negotiated if the subject is to achieve self-knowledge, salvation, mental health, bodily pleasure or control, and a variety of other objectives. The body of the subject is not so much shaped or brought into being by desire; rather, it is a palimpsest that records and re-records the imposed truths of power. As Butler writes:

Foucault's critique of the discourse on desire, on the figure of the 'subjects of desire', does well to remind us that desire is a name that not only accounts for an experience, but determines that experience as well, that the subject of desire may well be a fiction useful to a variety of regulatory strategies ... If the history of desire must be told in terms of the history of bodies, then it becomes necessary how that history encodes itself in these most immediate phenomena. (1987: 238)

Subjects of Desire is a book about Hegelian narratives and accounts of desire that ends on a very Nietzschean note: desire is posited as an element at play in the workings of power, specifically in terms of its role in the production of, and its relation to, the notions of subjectivity and identity.

SUBJECTION

After *Subjects of Desire*, Butler's most sustained and developed attempt to explain and identify what is at stake in this imbrication of desire, power, subjectivity and identity is to be found in *The Psychic Life of Power* (1997b). It is written largely from a Nietzschean and Foucaltian theoretical perspective, but it also seeks to build, or perhaps maintain, a bridge with the Freudian and Lacanian insights discussed in *Subjects of Desire* (and elaborated upon in *Gender Trouble* and *Bodies That Matter*).

Butler (1997b) refers to the situation where the subject is not only constituted through and dominated by, but also remains necessarily tied to and reliant on, the practices and discourses of power, as a form of 'subjection'. The point of this term is that it picks up on both sets of the aforementioned operations, and refuses the idea that the subject and any form of agency are not to some extent mediated by or negotiated through power and its various techniques (discourses, norms, forms of surveillance). Butler points out that power is thought of as something that is 'done to us', and which we seek to escape from or avoid:

But if, following Foucault, we understand power as forming the subject as well, as providing the very condition of its existence and the trajectory of its desire, then power is not simply what we oppose but also, in a strong sense, what we depend on for our existence and what we harbor and preserve in the beings that we are ... Subjection consists precisely in this fundamental dependency on a discourse we never chose but that, paradoxically, initiates and sustains our agency. (1997b: 2)

The issue that Butler identifies as the possible bridge between Foucault and psychoanalytical theory is the role of the psyche in the process. For Foucault subjects are brought into being by fitting into and gaining recognition in, and performing congruently with regard to, a discursive grid of intelligibility made up of normative categories, descriptions and narratives. Their place within this discursive space is maintained via techniques and operations of discipline and surveillance. The French historiographer and cultural theorist Michel de Certeau has written about how in a text such as *Discipline and Punish* (1995), Foucault produces a Freudian story of the 'vampirisation' of Enlightenment discourses (rationality, reason, progress, the teleological drive of human knowledge) by the apparatuses, techniques and mechanisms that provide the impetus for the development of 'penitential, educational and medical control at the beginning of the nineteenth century' (1988: 45). The relation between Enlightenment discourse and politics is not to be expressed as a dichotomy, but as a form of colonisation – disciplinary procedures take over the Enlightenment project, riding on the back of the ideology of revolution.

There are a number of aspects to Foucault's work on disciplinary procedures – 'This detective story about a substituted body' (Certeau 1988: 46) – that are of particular interest here. Although these procedures inhabit and feed off Enlightenment ideologies, they appear to have no discursive place of their own. Techniques spread themselves throughout social space to the extent that they, and not the contending ideologies of sovereignty or the revolution, triumph. Why do these disciplinary techniques 'win out' in the end? Certeau suggests that via the introduction of 'a cellular space of the same type for everyone (schoolboys, soldiers, workers, criminals or the ill) ... in order to make of it a tool capable of disciplining ... and "treating" any human group whatsoever' (1988: 46). What we have here is a set of techniques of observation, regulation and control that will culminate in what, for Foucault, is our contemporary system of power.

In works such as *The Order of Things* (1973) and *The Archaeology of Knowledge* (1972) Foucault demonstrates how these procedures feed back into, and are eventually articulated within and legitimated by, a variety of official discourses ('the human sciences') and 'optical and panoptical procedures which increasingly multiply ... and reproduce themselves little by little throughout all the strata of society' (Certeau 1988: 47). However what is largely missing from Foucault's accounts of disciplinarity and normalisation is a technical explanation of:

> how the subject is formed in submission. Not only does the entire domain of the psyche remain largely unremarked in his theory, but power in this double valence of subordinating and producing remains unexplored. Thus, if submission is a condition of subjection, it makes sense to ask: What is the psychic form that power takes? Such a project requires thinking the theory of power together with a theory of the psyche ... this present inquiry seeks to explore the provisional perspectives from which each theory illuminates the other. (Butler 1997b: 2–3)

The notion of the psyche playing a central role in the process of subjection is complicated by the theoretical problem of how it is able to perform this function, given that a psyche presumes (and requires) a subject in the first place. Butler points, by way of example, to the influential (1956) Nietzschean idea of consciousness turning – or being turned – back upon itself: consciousness confronts the other, which manifests itself as both a threat and an accusation, and inaugurates a psychic phenomenon of bad conscience whereby the subject accepts the authority of the other and directs violence against itself (in the form of guilt). This theory forms the basis of Louis Althusser's notion of the subject being interpellated into existence. In his influential essay 'Ideology and Ideological State Apparatuses', Althusser argues that institutions, texts and discourses recruit:

> subjects among the individuals ... or 'transforms' the individuals into subjects ... by interpellation or hailing ... which can be imagined among the lines of the most commonplace everyday police (or other) hailing: 'Hey, you there!' Assuming that the theoretical scene I have imagined takes place in the street, the hailed individual will turn round. By this mere one-hundred-and-eighty-degree physical conversion, he becomes a subject. Why? Because he has recognized that the hail was 'really' addressed to him. (1977: 163)

The analogy is straightforward enough: in Althusser's example it is a policeman shouting to someone in the street, but it could be a school teacher talking to a student in a classroom, or even a bureaucratic form that has to be filled out. When any authority addresses us and gets a response, in that moment the departure point or context of the encounter is the right of the authority figure to categorise, and the validity of the categorisation that is provided. This formulation is problematical to some extent, because it appears to leave out the possibility of any form of agency or disobedience: as Butler points out 'The law might not only be refused ... it might also be ruptured' and its 'monotheistic force' called into question (1993: 122). Althusser's point, however, is that it does not matter so much whether a subject 'believes' in authority and its self-narratives (the state knows best, the police are working in your interest, you should work harder, etc.). He refers to Pascal's famous dictum that if you 'Kneel down, move your lips in prayer ... you will believe' (1977: 158). What this means is that it is the ritual of call and response that in fact produces compliant subjects. Put simply, by acting as if we believe, we end up believing in what we act.

Nietzschean-influenced theories of subjection, within which Foucault's and Althusser's work can be grouped, all fail to account, however, for the problem of the psyche without a subject. Butler's response is to think of their accounts as tropological; that is to say, Foucault's normalisation, Nietzsche's bad conscience and Althusser's interpellation are read as a theoretical mechanism that 'facilitates ... [an] explanation but also marks its limits' (1997b: 4). This is what motivates Butler's interest in pursuing a connection with psychoanalysis. The idea of the subject as the product of a relation of parts and process (involving formation and subordination), that are both linear and simultaneous with regard to one another, more or less demands a mechanism that is congruent with the notions of repression and the unconscious:

> The Foucaltian postulation of subjection as the simultaneous subordination and forming of the subject assumes a specific psychoanalytical valence when we consider that no subject emerges without a passionate attachment to those on whom he or she is fundamentally dependent ... Although the dependency of the child is not political subordination in any usual sense, the formation of primary passion in dependency renders the child vulnerable to subordination and exploitation ... Moreover, this situation of primary dependence conditions the political formation and regulation of subjects and becomes the means of their subjection. (1997b: 7)

The notion of a 'passionate attachment' is what sets the psychoanalytical narrative of subjection in train, but it is an attachment that is always problematical and potentially scandalous; at best it is a point of tension, and at worst a scene of desire that threatens to unravel the subject. Just as with the process of anaclisis, where at a specific bodily level the site of attachment (literally, the nipple or breast as origin of the supply of milk) is transformed into something more than the instinctual, so the condition of the child's relation to its main carer (it need not be a parent) is initially one of necessity and survival. If the child is to persist it must become dependent, but the move from dependency to love is simultaneously dealt a violence that effectively splits the subject. This is what is meant, in the technical sense, by the notion of foreclosure: that which is constitutive of the subject is sent away and can only reappear to trigger the dissolution of the subject. As Butler points out, this is the real logic and condition of subjection, since 'To desire the condition of one's own subordination is thus required to persist as oneself' (1997b: 9).

How does Butler tie foreclosure to the Foucaltian processes of regulation, discipline and normalisation; or again, how are these practices and techniques incorporated by the subject at the level of the psyche? Psychoanalytical accounts refer to the internal workings of the subject (the psyche), while Foucault demonstrates how socio-cultural objectivities – spaces and architecture, discourses, the repetition of mechanisms of surveillance – produce compliant and docile (and productive) subjects-as-bodies. Butler argues that rather than considering these components as a relation of linearity – the psyche facilitating regulation and normalisation, or the other way around – it is more useful to consider them as two sides of the operation of power. As she writes:

> to the extent that norms operate as psychic phenomena, restricting and producing desire, they also govern the formation of the subject and circumscribe the domain of the livable sociality. The psychic operation of the norm offers a more insidious route for regulatory power than explicit coercion, one whose success allows its tacit operation within the social. (1997b: 21)

This imbrication of the psyche with mechanisms of discipline not only offers a technical explanation as to how the imperatives and logics – and violence – of power are internalised; it also goes some way to getting around the anti-historical bent of psychoanalysis; and perhaps even more importantly it provides something of an alternative to the structural closure of psychoanalytic accounts of the subject, by grounding it in social and historical processes and practices. What this means is that a gap is opened up between the rules and norms through which the subject is both constituted and disposed, and the discursive operation which produces the illusion of the universality and naturalisation of those norms. Moreover, Foucault maintains that what power produces is not necessarily in line with its aims, and indeed that it contains within it the seeds of its own vulnerability. While any sense of agency or political resistance can only take place within the terms of power, those terms are always predicated on a set of categories that are outside, and antithetical to, what is authorised and prescribed as the normal, healthy, and the recognisably human:

> being psychic, the norm does not merely reinstate social power, it becomes formative and vulnerable in highly specific ways. The social categorizations that establish the vulnerability of the subject ... are themselves vulnerable to psychic and historical change. This view counters an understanding of psychic or linguistic normativity ... that is prior to the social ... Just as the subject is derived from conditions of power that precede it, so the psychic operation of the norm is derived ... from prior social operations. (Butler 1997b: 21)

Exactly the same may be said of desire: it is not only regulated and disposed by power, but it is also facilitated by it, in ways quite contrary to normative logics and narratives. As Butler points out, through the act of prohibition the law inadvertently eroticises what it bars: at the moment that a particular path is denied me, it becomes 'the focus of desire' (1997b: 103). This is why, for Lacanian psychoanalysis, the prohibition against incest always works contrary to its intentions: it takes a potential relationship that has no intrinsic erotic or sexual potential on its own, and invests it with the status of a structural universality upon which society and culture are founded. So the universality of the law of incest prohibition is characterised by this mechanistic arbitrariness that undermines its own logic. The rule forecloses incestuous relations, but this only makes the idea of unthinkable incest all the more desirable. A good example of this can be seen in Pasolini's film *Oedipus Rex*, where the sexual tension and desire between the two main characters patently intensifies as the signs of the truth of their relationship proliferate. Oedipus and Jocasta act as if incest is foreclosed and unthinkable, but the fact of its foreclosure increases their desire to commit incest.

IDENTITY AND IDENTIFICATION

To this point we have dealt with most of the theoretical issues we identified from *Gender Trouble* and *Bodies That Matter* – the formation of the body as a culturally intelligible site and text, the status of desire and its relation to subjectivity, and the processes whereby the subject is simultaneously formed through and subjected to the regulatory regimes of power. What remains is the relation between subjectivity and the notion of identity (and by extension, identification), and the two sets of questions we posed earlier in this chapter: first, how can we distinguish identity from subjectivity; and second, to what extent can identity be said to facilitate or involve a sense of identification-as-agency?

Butler offers the clearest account of how she understands the first issue in the 'Introduction' to *The Psychic Life of Power*, where she seeks to explain the difference between the subject and the individual human body-as-identity. She writes that:

> The 'subject' is sometimes bandied about as if it were interchangeable with 'the person' or 'the individual'. The genealogy of the subject ... however, suggests that the subject, rather than being identified strictly with the individual, ought to be designated as a linguistic category, a placeholder, as structure in formation. Individuals come to occupy the site of the subject (the subject simultaneously emerges as a 'site') ... No individual becomes a subject without first becoming subjected. (1997b: 10–11)

Subjection, from this perspective, is understood as having a structural or architectural function: it both allows subjects to be (recognised); and provides them with an entry to, and a narrational trajectory within, the wider socio-cultural field.

For Butler the central form of identity is sexual identity: in order to preserve this identity, identification must be in accordance with the incest prohibition and the dictates of heteronormativity (this issue will be dealt with in detail in the following chapter). Identification, then, is not so much a kind of agency as a choice where there is no choice; the subject is designated by or called names (girl, child, daughter), and forms of attachment, and eventually, desire, must be recognisably and commensurably normal. Identification is also, crucially, about non-identification, both at the level of the incest prohibition and by extension, the prescribed narratives of sexuality. As Butler writes:

> It seems clear that the positions of 'masculine' and 'feminine' ... are established in part through prohibitions which demand the loss of certain sexual attachments, and demand as well that these losses not be avowed, and not be grieved ... The oedipal conflict presumes that heterosexual desire has already been

accomplished, that the distinction between heterosexual and homosexual has been enforced (a distinction which, after all, has no necessity); in this sense, the prohibition on incest presupposes the prohibition on homosexuality, for it presumes the heterosexualization of desire. (1997b: 135)

More generally, and across a variety of cultural fields, the subject both 'chooses' and achieves further identities. This involves developing literacy with regard to the requirements (discourses, performances, forms of value, bodily hexis) associated with each category and site of identity, and ensuring that the choices made are in keeping with normative values. We can think here of the process Bourdieu identifies whereby the habitus – which he refers to as 'history naturalized' – ensures that the choices made and values identified with are disposed, but that the fact of disposition is displaced to the level of the unconscious; in other words, disposition and necessity are misrecognised as free will or choice (Bourdieu 2000). For Bourdieu, cultural practices and choices are always the result of a coming together of the habitus and specific cultural fields and contexts. As people pass through various cultural fields and institutions, and come under their influence, they are disposed to regard those values, discourses, ideals and ways of doing things as natural and, to some extent, universal. As Butler writes 'This belief derives ... from the ideas of the individual concerned, i.e. from him as a subject with a consciousness which contains the ideas of his belief. In this way the ... attitude of the subject concerned naturally follows' (1997b: 210–11).

Bourdieu not only demonstrates 'how norms become embodied', he also 'offers a promising account of the way in which non-intentional and non-deliberate incorporations of norms take place' (Butler 1997b: 142). His analysis of the ongoing relation between subjects, objective structures, and time and place demonstrates that practices are explicable neither in terms of the institutional logics, narratives, rules, values, discourses and ideologies of a field (the objective conditions of practice), nor in terms of individual, unmediated decision making. The habitus is made up of a number of dispositions, modes of operation, inclinations, values and rationales. These principles:

> generate and organize practices and representations that can be objectively adapted to their outcomes without presupposing a conscious aiming at ends or an express mastery of the operations necessary in order to attain them. Objectively 'regulated' and 'regular' without being in any way the product of obedience to rules, they can be collectively orchestrated without being the product of the organizing action of a conductor. (Bourdieu 1990: 53)

Practices are the result, then, of the conjuncture – always slightly 'out of synch' – between the formative dispositions of the habitus, and the objective conditions that are produced out of these conjunctures. Butler characterises this process as a 'vector of temporalities' (2005: 35): quite simply, the time of the objectivities of any cultural field, and of the wider field and operations of power, is never synchronous with the time of any subject. Further, no subject is ever entirely in time with another, regardless of the levels or felicities of recognition, similarities of place, or a closely shared habitus. This is partly because the places that a subject occupies within a field or fields are never entirely substitutable with, or analogous to, another: the extent to which each subject is out of synch with regard to the field will vary from place to place, and consequently from subject to subject. As a corollary, there are also the questions of the extent to which some subjects are able to anticipate when and where a field is going, or which norms are in the process of being modified, and what is at stake in this modification and for whom, and what are the best ways of profiting from it? The gap between habitus and field can be productive to the extent that their lack of synchronicity can be the basis for their unravelling; in other words, where two strongly naturalised systems or logics mutually refute one another, a subject's 'unconscious belief' must be challenged on some level.

The disjunction between the life of the subject and the socio-cultural order of things is captured in Foucault's assertion that 'discourse is not your life, its time is not yours' (Burchill et al. 1991: 72). The subject is not only always out of time, however, but also affectively disconnected from, if not entirely irrelevant to, those orders of discourse (and the circulation of power) that purport to address the subject. As Foucault makes clear, a subject is always and necessarily alienated from the conditions that make being possible:

> Must I suppose that, in my discourse, it is not my own survival which is at stake? And that, by speaking, I do not exorcise my death, but establish it ... that I yield my utterance to an outside which is so indifferent to my life, so neutral, that it knows no difference between my life and my death? (Burchill et al. 1991: 71)

CONCLUSION

In a sense the subject is like the fabled man from the country in Kafka's *The Trial*, who continually seeks, but is refused admittance to, a door through which he will stand before the law, only to hear, 'at the end of his strength', that 'No one but you could gain admittance through this door, since this door was intended only for you. I am now going to shut it' (Kafka 1976: 237). His life is exhausted, metaphorically and literally, but at the same time it is the imperative to 'attain the law' that gives his life coherence, purpose, focus and direction. As Butler puts it, the norms that 'sustain my life in its intelligibility' both 'interrupt the time of my living' and are 'indifferent to me, to my life and my death', but 'Paradoxically, it is ... this disorientation ... this instance of an indifference ... that nevertheless sustains my living' (2005: 35). In the next chapter we will look at how these processes and issues are addressed in, and to some extent refracted by, Butler's various engagements with feminist theory.

FURTHER READING

Bourdieu, P. (2000) *Pascalian Meditations*. Cambridge: Polity Press.

Foucault, M. (2005) *The Hermeneutics of the Subject*. New York: Picador.

Nietzsche, F. (1956) *The Birth of Tragedy and The Genealogy of Morals*. New York: Doubleday Anchor.

2 Gender

INTRODUCTION

In *Gender Trouble* (1990) Butler examines the ways in which gender is understood and utilised in feminist theory. She draws attention to the persistent critique that within feminism the universalised subject of 'women' privileges the experiences of dominant groups within that category, and leaves unexamined the consequences of differences such as race or class (p. 14). Rather than seeking to articulate the means by which feminism might represent women more fully, Butler suggests that the very impetus to do so might in fact mask relations of power antithetical to any transformation of the relations and regulations of gender. Thus, she questions the dominant assumption in feminist theory that feminist politics should be a representational politics organised around the category of women, and suggests that 'it may be time to entertain a radical critique that seeks to free feminist theory from the necessity of having to construct a single or abiding ground' (p. 5).

Butler's critique centres on the mechanisms by which 'women' in feminist representational politics comes to assume the status of a stable, knowable and universal subject, an assumption that Butler contends is 'an unwitting regulation and reification of gender relations' (p. 5). What Butler means by this is that the category 'women' appears as though it has always been there as self-evident, when it is in fact a consequence of a productive field of power. Since that field of power produces inequities of gender, feminism's uncritical replication of women thus ensures that the mechanisms of power that produce gender oppression remain unscrutinised. Butler argues that rather than a strategy of representational politics, feminism would be better served by an enquiry into, and critique of, the terms by which the category of women comes to have any currency as a meaningful cultural category.

GENDER AND GENEALOGY

What she proposes in *Gender Trouble* is a 'genealogical critique' (1990: ix) of gender categories. The notion of genealogy that Butler uses follows the work of Foucault (who draws on the work of Nietzsche). As we saw in the previous chapter, Foucault argues that genealogy must be utilised to examine 'what we tend to feel is without history' (1991: 76) because of the way it appears to function as universal. Rather than seeking an overarching origin to the institutions or paradigms that circulate as self-evident or universal, genealogy examines the interplays of power and knowledge that produce both the institution, and the means by which it circulates as universal.

For example, in volume one of *The History of Sexuality* (2008), Foucault examines how heterosexuality came to be understood as a form of sexuality distinct from homosexuality, while simultaneously being constituted as the universal norm from which 'the homosexual' deviates. Foucault asserts that prior to the end of the eighteenth century sodomy was regarded primarily in a juridical frame as 'against the law', differing only in terms of degrees of 'naturalness' (pp. 38–40) from other sins such as extramarital relations or adultery. However, following a 'centrifugal movement with respect to heterosexual monogamy' (pp. 38–9) in which heterosexuality was enacted under a new discourse of privacy, and an increasingly public focus on the people who participated in the non-normative aspects of sexuality, sexual deviancy became both compelled to speak, and intimately attached to the bodies that spoke it. Foucault cites numerous examples of this 'incitement to discourse' around acts of perversity, from the church confessional to the psychiatrist's couch. As this discourse of perversity developed, a new 'specification of individuals' (p. 43) became intimately linked with the perversions in which those individuals engaged, and the notion of an identifiable homosexual emerged. Whereas homosexuality was now constituted as an identity, heterosexuality was simultaneously required to speak of itself 'less and less' (p. 38). Heterosexuality thus appears as being 'without history', when that very appearance is dependent upon subjectivating discursive practices emerging within a field of power. Butler wishes to approach gender in a similar way, by conducting 'a feminist genealogy of the category of women' (1990: 5) that will trace the mechanisms of power by which 'women' comes to appear as though it has no constitutive history.

SEX AND GENDER

What frames this genealogical approach is Butler's critique of the distinction between 'sex' and 'gender' that is utilised in some feminist theory. The sex/gender distinction separates the biological givens that differentiate bodies into male and female from the cultural specificities that those bodies are naturalised to assume. It owes a particular debt to Gayle Rubin's (1975) essay 'The Traffic in Women: Notes on the "Political Economy" of Sex'. Rubin argues that the Marxist framework that dominates analyses of social inequity (including feminism) fails to 'fully express or conceptualise sex oppression' (p. 160). Paraphrasing Marx's observation that resources of production only become capital under certain social conditions, Rubin argues that a woman 'only becomes a domestic, a wife, a chattel, a playboy bunny, a prostitute, or a human Dictaphone in certain relations' (p. 158). That is, certain relations transform the 'biological raw material of human sex and procreation' (p. 165) into the limited range of subject positions available to women. Rubin terms this set of arrangements the 'sex/gender system', where sex is understood as the 'biological raw' of anatomy and gender as the 'certain relations' (p. 159) that transform it. According to Rubin the social relations of gender that underpin this system cannot be fully explained by Marxism alone.

Butler draws on a number of aspects of 'The Traffic in Women', and we will discuss that use later in the chapter. Her analysis of the ways in which women are produced differs from Rubin's, however, with regard to the assumption of a biological raw material that somehow precedes the cultural arrangements it is forced to undergo. In her genealogical approach, Butler is interested in how feminist analysis that pulls apart that process of naturalisation tends to leave an unexamined notion of the body in place. Butler's critique centres primarily on the ways in which the body is repeatedly imagined as existing prior to the discursive field that it is produced within. Whereas the sex/gender distinction draws attention to the material fact of sex, Butler argues that the truth of sex, along with the suggestion that such a thing exists, is produced via the same regulatory practices that produce the norms of gender (1990: 17). Thus Butler wants to ask: 'To what extent does the body come into being in and through the mark(s) of gender?' (p. 8).

A discussion Butler undertakes in *Undoing Gender* (2004) offers a useful way of understanding what she means by this. In the essay 'Undiagnosing Gender', Butler examines the contradictions and complications for transgender people regarding the way in which Gender Identity Disorder (GID) is utilised to 'diagnose' one's need/desire to surgically transform the signs of gender. Given the cost of gender-related surgery and hormone regimes, the capacity to be diagnosed, and thus render such treatment non-elective, makes gender intervention relatively affordable. Of course the 'payoff', as Butler notes, is that one is subject to, and subjectivated by, a discourse of pathologisation in a quite possibly transphobic context (2004: 76). The range of issues that this raises is complex, but of particular relevance to the present discussion is the way in which Butler describes how the hierarchies of gender intervention produced by GID demonstrate the contradictions inherent in the material notion of sex.

Butler refers the example of a butch lesbian diagnosed with breast cancer. The cancer necessitated the removal of one of her breasts; however she decided to have a full mastectomy in order to lessen the risk of the cancer recurring. As Butler describes it 'The choice was made easier for her because she had no strong emotional attachment to her breasts: they did not form an important part of her gendered or sexual self-understanding' (pp. 85–6). Concerned that they would be setting a precedent for what they considered elective transsexual surgery, however, her insurance company was reluctant to fund the second mastectomy. In order to qualify for insurance, she could have presented as trans in order to be diagnosed with GID, yet Butler points to the range of gendered bodily transformations routinely undertaken as enhancements of gender that are never imagined or articulated in psychiatric discourse. What Butler draws attention to in her discussion of this is the range of paradoxes and contradictions that surround the options both available and unavailable to the butch as a consequence, and the ways in which those limits are set to reflect normative expectations of one's relationship to sex characteristics.

Butler argues that the range of acceptability in terms of gendered body modification is routinely aligned with the normative expectations of gender. This ranges from penile enhancements or breast surgeries, to decisions about hair length or body size. In perhaps her clearest articulation of precisely why sex thus cannot be imagined as materially true, Butler argues:

> Yet these practices [haircuts and diets] are part of the daily habits of cultivating secondary sex characteristics, if that category is taken to mean all the various bodily indicators of sex. If the bodily traits 'indicate' sex, then sex is not quite the same as the means by which it is indicated. Sex is made understandable through

the signs that indicate how it should be read or understood. These bodily indicators are the cultural means by which the sexed body is read. They are themselves bodily, and they operate as signs, so there is no easy way to distinguish between what is 'materially' true, and what is 'culturally' true about a sexed body. I don't mean to suggest that purely cultural signs produce a material body, but only that the body does not become sexually readable without those signs, and that those signs are irreducibly cultural and material at once. (2004: 87)

Thus sex as a material or embodied difference between male and female only has meaning within the cultural framework that in the sex/gender distinction it is otherwise imagined to precede. To render it distinct would be to suggest that a body read through either gender would appear in exactly the same way in either reading.

This is the position that Butler argues Rubin adopts in 'The Traffic in Women' (Rubin & Butler 1997). Among the social relations of gender that Rubin examines are the kinship arrangements that Claude Lévi-Strauss argues are produced through the exchange of women. In order to change the meanings attached to female bodies as a consequence of this, Rubin advocates the removal or transformation of kinship arrangements. Overthrowing the system of kinship would simultaneously remove the 'cultural residue and the symbolic manifestations and all of the other aspects of that system, and the inscription and installation of those structures and categories within people' (1997: 72). To put it more simply, removing existing kinship structures would remove the system of gender. Under such a transformation sex difference would appear to entirely different effect within culture, and bodies could proceed 'without reference to gender disparity' (Butler 1990: 75). Butler argues that this is a utopian vision – a point with which Rubin in a later interview agrees (Rubin & Butler 1997: 72) – that posits gender as a 'free-floating artifice' (Butler 1990: 6) thoroughly independent of sex. The logical conclusion of this, she asserts, is that there is no necessity that 'the construction of "men" will accrue exclusively to the bodies of males or that "women" will only interpret female bodies' (p. 6). Any body could exhibit any gender, and maintain the integrity of its sexed embodiment. Yet what culture repeatedly makes clear, and what Butler seeks to draw attention to, is that a failure to conform to gender norms does not leave an unproblematically sexed body in place. Rather, such a failure is precisely what calls the legitimacy of the body into question. As Butler argues, those bodies that do not cohere between sex and gender function as unintelligible at the level of the body, the very materiality of which is repeatedly articulated as indisputable.

LEGIBLE BODIES

An example that demonstrates this in the terms that Butler describes is the attention paid to Caster Semenya, the South African athlete who won gold in the women's 800 metres at the 2009 World Athletics Championships. Despite being identified as a girl at birth and raised as such, and having competed as a woman throughout her career, the 'masculinity' of Semenya's appearance (her face, voice, physique), along with the speed with which she had risen through the ranks of international athletics, cast doubt on the legitimacy of her gender identity. Following the World Championships she was required by the International Association of Athletics Federations (IAAF) to undergo gender testing before her medal title would be confirmed. A discourse of privacy surrounds the nature of that testing, but according to a *TIME* magazine report it involves 'an endocrinologist, a gynaecologist, a psychologist, and both internal and external examinations' (Adams 2009). Early media speculation pointed to an excess of testosterone as the likely explanation for Semenya's deviation from the norms of gender; however a number of reports also claimed that the testing had revealed Semenya to be intersex. As of November 2009, the IAAF have stated that as a consequence of the tests Semenya will retain her world title, but that the results of the testing will not be publicly released. In announcing the decision, the South African sports ministry stated that Semenya had been found 'innocent of any wrong' (*Guardian* 2009), which commentators have interpreted to mean that there is no evidence of deliberate gender cheating, but that this may not necessarily mean Semenya qualifies as a woman for the purposes of competition (Epstein 2009).

The institutional and media responses to Semenya raise a myriad of issues around (among other things) intersex, gender normativity, the relationships between gender and class, and especially between gender and race. For the purposes of our discussions here, it also highlights how intelligibility functions in relation to gender; what that intelligibility means for the relationship between sex and gender; and what the ramifications are when a body is rendered unintelligible within this paradigm of identity. As we noted, Butler argues that the notion of gender as 'radically independent of sex' (1990: 6) presumes that any gender may accrue to any body. Yet it is the integrity of Semenya's sex that is called into question and subject to a range of unspecified tests, not because an anomaly was discovered in the usual markers of sex (genitalia), but because her gender performance was at odds with a sex already noted and registered at birth. As Butler notes in her analysis of David Reimer (discussed in the previous chapter), a body's verifiability is subject to an ongoing regime of scrutiny. Given the range of experts seemingly called in to assess Semenya, she (like David) is subjected to a 'normalizing ideal ... conveyed through a plurality of gazes', all repeating a question that belies the naturalness of sex: 'is this person feminine enough' (Butler 2004: 67)? Were gender a free-floating cultural attachment such a question would not need to be asked, and thus what is revealed is that the cultural intelligibility of sex requires sex and gender to cohere (and to continue to cohere) in a particular, and normative, way.

One consequence of the media discussion of Semenya has been to highlight the extensive array of anatomical/hormonal/chromosomal variations within apparently self-evident gender categories. At the same time, that discussion tends inevitably to frame such anomalies with an expectation that variations, once discovered, should be corrected. David Epstein, writing online for *Sports Illustrated* (2009), suggests that if Semenya were found to have three times the level of testosterone considered normal for a woman (as was reported elsewhere to be the case), such a finding would 'indicate a medical problem that requires treatment'. Much like the *TIME* headline that asks 'Could This Women's World Champ Be a Man?' (Adams 2009), what this demonstrates is an inability to conceive of a discussion that goes beyond deciding which of the two existing gender categories this body will be made to be intelligible within. Such an impetus belies the assertion that sex comes first, and that gender is culturally inscribed onto an otherwise unmarked body, and demonstrates instead Butler's argument that it is the discursive framework of gender that produces sex. Thus the understanding that sex is a straightforward anatomical difference is an understanding that is the effect of gender. Butler argues that:

> gender is not to culture as sex is to nature; gender is also the discursive/cultural means by which 'sexed nature' or 'a natural sex' is produced and established as 'prediscursive', prior to culture, a politically neutral surface on which culture acts. (1990: 7)

As Butler puts it, sex turns out to 'have been gender all along' (p. 8), because it is via the way in which gender is understood as cultural that the sexed body is able to masquerade as anatomical fact. Thus, to some degree, the sex/gender distinction still makes sense, but not in the terms of the nature/culture dichotomy that Butler argues dominates feminist theory. Rather, sex is sexual difference (the distinction between men and women) but it is sexual difference understood as a discursively produced organising framework. Gender is the process (social, cultural, economic, political) by which sex comes to appear as though it is a materially different thing from the gendering processes that render it intelligible.

Thus Butler argues that the '"coherence" and "continuity" of "the person" are not logical or analytic features of personhood, but, rather socially instituted and maintained norms of intelligibility' (1990: 7). Nonetheless, those bodies that fail to cohere within those norms are simultaneously excluded from the recognition as persons that coherence to those norms confers. As she states repeatedly across her work, the stakes of cultural intelligibility, and the recognition it confers, are high. In the anniversary edition of *Gender Trouble* (1999), she locates the 'violence of gender norms' firmly within the kind of material life her critics contend she ignores, and speaks, for example, of 'an uncle incarcerated for his anatomically anomalous body' (1999: xix). In *Undoing Gender* (2004) she argues that the norms by which humanness is understood are also the terms by which human rights and political participation are conferred. Those norms are attached to the categorisation of identity, and the verification of belonging to that identity. Thus Butler argues that the 'human is understood differentially depending on its race, the legibility of that race, its morpohology, the recognizability of that morphology, its sex, the perceptual verification of that sex' (2004: 2). In as much as a belonging to a race other than white, or a sex other than male, positions a body as the lesser of two parts of any binary, a failure to be recognisable as either term in such a dualism positions a body on an entirely different register of viability. Repeated over and again in the coverage of Caster Semenya was the question of whether she was a 'real' woman, the question that the IAAF sought to settle. It is this calling into question of one's reality that, for Butler, belies critiques of the material effect of discourse because 'to be called unreal, and to have that call, as it were, institutionalized as a form of differential treatment, is to become the other against which the human is made' (2004: 218).

Butler's insistence, in the work that follows *Gender Trouble,* on the ramifications of illegibility, was partly a response to a persistent feminist critique that in asserting that the sexed body is produced through discourse, she ignores the materiality of the body. Within such arguments, Butler asserts, matter is taken to be the indisputable biology of difference, the bodies that 'live and die; eat and sleep; feel pain, pleasure; endure illness and violence' (1993: xi). It is these bodies that critics contend 'cannot be dismissed as mere construction' (p. xi). Rather than disputing this irrefutability, Butler instead draws attention to how the notion of construction in such critiques is understood. She argues that to define the body as a construction, as she does, is not to render it either artificial or false; rather it is to hold that bodies only make sense, only come to be understood, through a variety of descriptive regimes. In one sense, bodies only appear through the language we have to describe them. It is through the way bodies are described or spoken that they become intelligible, and it is in this description that bodies are constructed. Butler uses the moment of birth as an example of this. She argues that when a baby is born, the attribution of a gender pronoun transforms that baby from the inhuman 'it' (as in 'What is it?') to the she or he ('It's a girl!') that renders the infant intelligible (p. 7). In this interpellative moment, the phrase 'It's a girl' only makes sense because there is an understanding of 'girl' that precedes it, and that requires its ongoing adherence.

This latter point – that construction is not a singular act – is a critical one for Butler. She argues that discussions around construction tend to become mired in issues of agency, where the question becomes: 'If gender is a construction, must there be an "I" or a "we" who enacts or performs that construction?' (1993: 7); or, in claims that structures such as 'Culture or Discourse or Power' (p. 9) pre-empt human agency and engender the constructivist act. In either account, Butler argues, construction is conceived of in singular terms, as either productive of a singular subject that through gendering is made recognisably human (p. 8), or as an act 'which happens once and whose effects are firmly fixed' (p. 9). As Caster Semenya demonstrates, however, the nominally descriptive moment of birth merely begins the process of 'girling'. A body must continue to adhere to, and be recognisable within, normative discourse to sustain that status of 'girl' (pp. 7–8). Moreover, the first description and all subsequent authorisations of that description, all of which we could describe as 'gender testing', repeat and reiterate the frameworks of intelligibility that precede the singularity of that body. As we discussed in the previous chapter, Butler seeks to shift discussions of sex from positions for and against constructivism, to an account of how matter materialises through the discursive means by which it appears to be organised and described. Butler thus reconceives matter 'not as a site or surface but as *a process of materialization that stabilizes over time to produce the effect of boundary, fixity, and surface we call matter*' (p. 9, emphasis in original).

THE MATERIALISATION OF SEX

In order to articulate how this process of materialisation takes place, Butler begins by working through the accounts of other theorists of sex construction. In *Gender Trouble* (and, indeed, throughout her discussion of gender) she utilises and critiques the work of Simone de Beauvoir, Monique Wittig, Luce Irigaray and Foucault, all of whom contend, in often radically different ways, that sex is produced within a field of power. Butler begins with Beauvoir, whose argument that 'one is not born a woman, but, rather, becomes one' (Beauvoir 1973: 301) seems the archetypal statement of construction. As she notes, Butler has drawn on Beauvoir's claim that 'the body is a situation' (p. 38) to conclude that 'there is no recourse to a body that has not always already been interpreted by cultural meanings' (1990: 8), a position that seems to support her own. Yet in *Gender Trouble* Butler qualifies that account by critiquing what she describes as Beauvoir's commitment to the Cartesian mind/body dualism. In Beauvoir's analysis of how the framework of male/female works, she argues that the male subject is always imagined as the universal subject, with the female positioned as his perpetual Other. The existential male subject thus assumes a status analogous to the rational mind, whereas the female remains mired in embodiment. As Butler notes 'the cultural associations of mind with masculinity and body with femininity are well documented within the field of philosophy and feminism' (1990: 12). In reproducing that split, Beauvoir thus imports the 'implicit gender hierarchy' (1990: 12) of the distinction, as well as a theory of embodiment that belies Butler's earlier interpretation of a discursively constructed body. As Nikki Sullivan explains, in the dualism of mind/body the body is imagined as 'a material receptacle that houses the mind or spirit' (2003: 41). Butler disputes any philosophical position in which the body is 'figured as a mere *instrument* or *medium*' external to cultural meanings, and insists, instead, that '"the body" is itself a construction' (Butler 1990: 8, emphasis in original).

For Irigaray, it is not that women are inferior, but rather that women do not signify at all within representative systems. The 'second sex' that the title of Beauvoir's famous work describes does not exist, and cannot exist, because the persistent association of women with the body always excludes them from the realm of subjectivity. Because women cannot be thought of in cultural terms, they only exist in culture as some kind of unformed or deformed version of masculinity. Thus, as Butler summarises, 'women represent the sex that cannot be thought, a linguistic absence and opacity' (1990: 9), and moments in which they seem to appear, as Butler puts it, are 'precisely the site of their erasure' (1993: 37). Thus, women function as a 'constitutive outside' (1993: 35) that produces the definitional limits of what can be thought – and what can be thought is always and only masculine. Butler sees Irigaray's attention to the masculinism of the signifying economy as a means of opening up the ways in which sex difference might be discussed. She argues that Irigaray 'makes clear that sexual difference is not a fact', but rather a product of the organising structures of language, a persistent question that remains 'unsettled and unresolved' (Butler 2004: 177). As we shall see, the political project that Butler lays out in *Gender Trouble* is one that seeks to utilise and exploit the irresolvable nature of the discursive reproduction of gender, and to that end there are productive intersections between her work and the instability of the signifying system that Irigaray describes (most notably in *Bodies That Matter* (1993)).

Yet Butler also argues that Irigaray, at times, falls back on a universalising notion of the materiality of sexual difference that is seemingly at odds with the position outlined above. Irigaray's description of the sex which is not 'one' refers both to the impossibility of women being a sex, but also to the impossibility of that sex being singular. The phallogocentric language system that only represents men, can only represent in univocal terms because singularity is the discourse of masculinity. For Irigaray, femaleness is multiple and could thus never be contained within this system. The only possibility that Irigaray sees of 'escaping the "mark" of gender', according to Butler (1990: 26), is the production of an alternative signifying economy. Yet, as Monique Wittig argues, this paradigm relies on a seemingly essentialised sexual difference (p. 26). Butler contends that by deploying a notion of femaleness in these terms, Irigaray tends toward a universalising framework of women. As a consequence, Butler argues, Irigaray risks 'colonizing under the sign of the same those differences that might otherwise call the totalizing concept into question' (p. 13).

Furthermore (and as an example, perhaps, of precisely that universalising gesture), while Beauvoir and Irigaray examine the ways in which women signify or otherwise in relation to men, neither pays critical attention to the ways in which their analysis of sex is structured by an implicit heterosexual binary. Wittig, in contrast, argues that the entire signifying system of male and female can only be conceived of in relation to what she terms the 'heterosexual economy' (1983: 66). Like Irigaray, Wittig argues that the category of sex is a purely linguistic construction, but she also contends that it is a construction that 'has meaning only in heterosexual systems of thought and heterosexual economic systems' (1980: 110). Wittig defines sex as 'a political category that founds society as heterosexual' (1983: 66), and that allows men to socially and economically enslave women. As sex can only be conceived of in heterosexual terms, Wittig concludes that lesbians are therefore 'not women' (1980: 110) because they sit outside the economy that gives that term its meaning.

For Wittig, the only possibility of transforming the status of women is the removal of the system of sex, thus enabling the emergence of a polymorphous sexuality that is not organised around any cognisance of genital difference. Because lesbians exist independent of men, and are thus not included in the economy of sex, they offer the possibility of 'an alternative economy of pleasures' (Butler 1990: 26) to that defined by what Wittig (a Marxist) sees as the economics attached to women's capacity to reproduce. As such, lesbians also demonstrate both the possibility and the means of overthrowing the system of sex. Because there is no inside of the system of sex that is not implicated in the inequities of compulsory heterosexuality (remember that for Wittig this is definitive of sex), the only options that she sees in relation to sex are, as Butler puts it, '(a) radical conformity or (b) radical revolution' (1990: 121).

Butler disagrees with Wittig on a number of key points. She argues that Wittig's characterisation of a polymorphous sexuality that will emerge in the wake of the dismantling of sex is based on a humanist notion of a 'pregendered "person", characterized as freedom' (1990: 20). For Butler any recourse to such a model of subjectivity is an effect of discourse, rather than its precursor. Butler also contends that Wittig seems to privilege heterosexuality as 'the only compulsory display of power that informs sexuality' (1990: 121–2). More critically (and informing both of the preceding positions), the model of resistance based around the idealised lesbian posits a place or mode of subjectivity that is outside the system of sex. Within this account two things are imagined that Butler wishes to question. First lesbian sexuality appears to circulate unfettered by the gendering impetus of heteronormativity. Second, compulsory heterosexuality can be overthrown by subjects no longer implicated within (or prior to) its subjectivating practices.

For Butler, Wittig's strategies of resistance misread the structure (and perhaps the force) of heteronormative power. In *Gender Trouble* Butler reflects upon the difficulty for feminism of articulating and enacting a resistive response to power that functions within, and against, the constraining systems of identity that she critiques. She contends that resisting power from within the field that it establishes is the only possible option. Any imagining outside of that field of power is an effect of power, a fantasy of agency that only serves to reaffirm what it would ostensibly oppose. As Butler puts it:

> If sexuality is culturally constructed within existing power relations, then the postulation of a normative sexuality that is 'before', 'outside', or 'beyond' power is a cultural impossibility and a politically impracticable dream, one that post-pones the concrete and contemporary task of rethinking subversive possibilities for sexuality and identity within the terms of power itself. (1990: 30)

It is from this model of power that Butler's critique of the sex/gender distinction is developed, and it is this working of power that this critique demonstrates. Butler also contends that just as the fantasy of a prediscursive sex is produced and naturalised through the operation of gender, so too is Wittig's notion of a lesbian 'radically unconditioned by heterosexual norms' (1990: 121) an effect of heteronormative discourse. The model of resistance that Wittig articulates is thus, for Butler, a cultural impossibility. In order to examine what model of resistance Butler would articulate instead, and what a 'within, and against' strategy in relation to identity might look like, we need firstly to examine the network of power that Butler argues sex is produced within.

THE HETERONORMATIVITY OF SEX

The conceptualising of the field of power in which sex is produced as radically heteronormative is a position that Butler firmly shares with Wittig, even if her strategies of intervention differ. We have already seen that for Butler the way in which the sex/gender distinction is routinely articulated in feminist theory is at odds with the ways in which norms of intelligibility refuse some bodies the status of the imagined material reality of sex. The category of 'women' relies on the coherence of sex and gender, a sanction that is often either masked or reaffirmed in feminist representational strategies. Critically, Butler locates the 'political reasons for the substantializing view of gender' within the requirements and regulations of a 'compulsory and naturalized heterosexuality' that she argues produces the binary gender system and its insistence on the 'internal coherence of sex, gender, and desire' (1990: 22–3). The unified subject of feminist theory is thus viable only if feminism fails to take account of the relationship between compulsory heterosexuality and the production of gender. A key impetus in the writing of *Gender Trouble* was Butler's wish to intervene in what she describes, to Liz Kotz, as the 'deep heterosexism of most feminist theory' (Kotz 1992: 83). Thus, among the most important questions she asks in that text is 'To what extent does the category of women achieve stability and coherence only in the context of the heterosexual matrix?' (Butler 1990: 5). Butler defines the 'heterosexual matrix' as 'that grid of cultural intelligibility through which bodies, genders, and desires are naturalized' (p. 151). Within that matrix, bodies only make sense (and only count as bodies that matter) when sex, gender and desire cohere within a framework structured by heterosexuality.

In her insistence that sex and gender cannot be thought outside of a regime of compulsory heterosexuality, and in her articulation of the form that power takes, Butler draws, in particular, on Foucault's work. At the end of the first volume of *The History of Sexuality*, after imagining the range of critiques that might be directed at his sustained account of the production of sexuality, Foucault turns his attention more fully to the imagined factity of sex. Like Butler, he is unwilling to accept an idea of a sex that exists in and of itself, and asks whether sex is 'really the anchorage point that supports the manifestations of sexuality, or is it not rather a complex idea that was formed inside the deployment of sexuality?' (Foucault 2008: 152). Foucault refuses to divest the production of sex from the regulation and subjection of sexuality that his *History* sets out, a subjection that naturalises heterosexuality. He contends that the science of sexuality, along with the juridical, economic and pedagogical practices of power that order and articulate desire, does so in ways that are indissociable from the sexed subject. Foucault's genealogical approach seeks to demonstrate how categories of sex work to conceal the very mechanism of their production, by naturalising sex as the origin of the generative regime of sexuality. As Butler puts it, the 'tactical production of the discrete and binary categorization of sex conceals the strategic aims of that very apparatus of production by postulating "sex" as "a cause" of sexual experience, behavior, and desire' (1990: 23).

The journals of the nineteenth-century hermaphrodite, Herculine Barbin (Foucault 1980a), demonstrate for both Foucault and Butler the ways in which bodies that cannot be ordered in the generative framework of heteronormative sexuality, simultaneously produce and demonstrate the limits *of* the cultural ordering of sex/gender/desire. If, as Elizabeth Grosz suggests, 'the body is what it is capable of doing, and what any body is capable of doing is well beyond the tolerance of any given culture' (1995: 214), then Barbin appears to reveal that the boundaries of tolerance are maintained by the refusal to count such bodies as legitimate social subjects (and here we might recall our earlier discussion of Caster Semenya). Yet Butler argues that such bodies might also disturb the naturalised framework that appears to refuse those bodies in the first place. Thus the scandal of Barbin is not that s/he disturbs the binary system of sexuality and sex, but rather that s/he threatens to call into question the linguistic and, for Butler, the performative, moves by which those systems are able to proliferate undisturbed in their everyday regulation of every other body.

GENDER PERFORMATIVITY

In the first chapter of *Gender Trouble,* in a section entitled 'Gender: The Circular Ruins of a Contemporary Debate', Butler asks 'Is there "a" gender which persons are said *to have,* or is it an essential attribute that a person is said *to be*' (1990: 7, emphasis in original). The title of the section suggests that for Butler neither question leads to a useful intervention. Instead, for Butler gender is not a question of having or of being, but of doing, and it is something one is compelled to do in order to be constituted as a recognisable human subject. Gender is a culturally sanctioned performance, a requirement that a body coheres, and continues to cohere, according to certain norms of intelligibility. The thesis of *Gender Trouble,* and the central concept on which Butler's theorisation of gender rests, is that gender is performative, and that the authority on which that performativity depends comes from the constitution of bodies within a heteronormative matrix of intelligibility. Butler's account of gender performativity draws on J.L. Austin's theory of linguistic performativity, and on the response to Austin by Derrida. Although neither Austin nor Derrida is mentioned in any significant detail in *Gender Trouble,* Butler's indebtedness to them (and to Derrida in particular) becomes explicit in *Bodies That Matter* (1993).

In *How To Do Things With Words* (1962), Austin observed that 'for too long' philosophers had assumed that 'the business of a "statement" can only be to "describe" some state of affairs, or to "state some fact", which it must do either truly or falsely' (p. 1). His analysis of the linguistic performative sought to shift such discussions away from claims and counterclaims in relation to veracity and truth, and toward discussions of how things come to be true via announcements that enact particular constitutive powers. As Derrida notes of Austin, it is enquiries into the 'value of force' rather than the 'value of truth' (1982: 322) that characterise his analysis of the performative. To that end, Austin demonstrated that certain utterances, in particular those connected to juridical citation, enact the very actions they describe. In such performative statements or speech acts, 'the issuing of the utterance is the performing of an action' (1962: 6). Among the examples Austin uses to demonstrate how performatives work is the marriage ceremony's 'I now pronounce you ...', legal proceedings' 'I sentence you ...' (1970: 235), and the contracting of a wager by way of 'I bet you ...' (1962: 7). All are examples of acts of speech that do as they say they are doing it.

What Derrida argues is that critical to the performative force of these utterances is the extent to which they explicitly or implicitly cite the power that enables them to produce their words as action. In the marriage example that Austin uses, the celebrant might precede the performative pronouncement with 'By the power vested in me by', and cite the appropriate inaugurating authority. Similarly the judge announcing 'I now sentence you' either cites the civil authority directly, or implicitly cites its performative weight through the robes and the other courtroom symbols of judicial authority. This mechanism of citation is an iteration of a previous phrase or set of conventions that establish the authority of the person citing them to enact what they describe, an authority that not every speaker has. The importance of this for Derrida is that it locates the speaker within an existing framework of authority, and thus forces the recognition that the power of the speaker's words do not originate within the speaker, but rather from the codes and conventions that the speaker finds his or herself within. Any performative is identifiable with, and conforms to, an iterable model (Derrida 1988), and in the act of citation the authority of that model is simultaneously reconstituted. The judge who cites the authority of the law in sentencing reminds the subject thus sentenced, and all other subjects, that the law gives him or her the power to do so.

For Butler, gender performativity operates through precisely the same logic of repetition and citation, and it is on these two functions that the efficacy of any performance of gender depends. She argues that certain announcements of gender, and certain performances of gender, produce the status and fixity of gender through the forced reiteration of norms. Discourses enact their own performatives by appearing to name that which they in fact produce through a reiteration of the constraints set up in the terms of that discourse. The truth of discourses of gender relies on markers of truth that are in fact produced by those discourses. That truth is enacted through the means by which:

> acts, gestures and desire produce the effect of an internal core or substance, but produce this *on the surface of the body* ... Such acts, gestures, enactments, generally construed, are *performative* in the sense that the essence or identity that they otherwise purport to express are *fabrications* manufactured and sustained through corporeal signs and other discursive means. (1990: 136, emphasis in original)

Thus the naturalness of 'being female' (or male) is constituted through 'discursively constrained performative acts that produce the body through and within the categories of sex' (1990: vii). The process of 'girling' that we discussed earlier begins with what seems like a moment of recognition ('It's a girl'), but is in fact an act of constitution ('This body must remain recognisable in these terms in order to continue to be accorded this status'). Subjectivity, and thus its limits, are bestowed as they are announced: 'Subjected to gender, but subjectivated by gender, the "I" neither precedes nor follows the process of this gendering, but emerges only within and as the matrix of gender relations themselves' (Butler 1993: 7). The bestowal of gender is not the founding of gender in each discrete moment, but rather a repetitive constitution that 'both conceals itself and enforces its rules' (Butler 1990: 145) as it produces them. Butler argues that the performativity that sustains the sex/gender system produces and naturalises sex with just as much discursive effect as it naturalises gender. The discursive operation of power that enacts gender norms does not do so onto a previously unmarked material body, as the materiality of that body is produced and sustained through the same discursive function of performativity.

Butler argues that the series of 'demands, taboos, sanctions, injunctions, prohibitions, impossible idealizations, and threats' that constitute the position of gender in discourse function to produce 'culturally viable sexual subjects' (1993: 106) through performative acts dependent on citationality. In *Bodies That Matter*, she refines her model of gender performativity by paying particular attention to the Derridean emphasis on citation. Butler's strategy here, in part, is to address what she describes as a 'bad reading' of the model of gender performance that seemed to proliferate in response to *Gender Trouble*. As Butler puts it in the Liz Kotz interview, the:

> bad reading goes something like this: I can get up in the morning, look in my closet, and decide which gender I want to be today. I can take out a piece of clothing and change my gender: stylize it, and then that evening I can change it again and be some radically other. (Kotz 1992: 83)

In *Bodies That Matter*, Butler draws on Derrida's emphasis on iterability to argue unequivocally that gender cannot be thought, understood, or experienced within these voluntarist terms.

As we established earlier, the phrase 'It's a girl' only has meaning because there is a framework of intelligibility that precedes and, crucially for Butler, requires that announcement. Thus, the arrival of a subject takes place within a network of meaning that has a long and established history of citation. For Derrida, it is this history of citation – where any citation echoes past citations – that gives a performative its force. Thus, he asks:

> Could a performative utterance succeed if its formulation did not repeat a 'coded' or iterable utterance, in other words, if the formula I pronounce in order to open a meeting, launch a ship or a marriage were not identifiable as conforming with an iterable model, if it were not then identifiable in some as a 'citation'? (1982: 18)

Butler uses this framework to argue that every performance of gender is required by the histories of gender intelligibility to cite the norms that precede and produce it, and that the ongoing requirement of gender performance requires the ongoing and repeated citations of those norms. Every girl is:

> compelled to 'cite' the norm in order to qualify and remain a viable subject. Femininity is thus not the product of a choice, but the forcible citation of a norm, one whose complex historicity is indissociable from relations of discipline, regulation, punishment. (1993: 232)

Butler argues that the naturalisation of gender performativity also naturalises and privileges heterosexuality. Gender norms and prohibitions produce a gender identity 'along the culturally intelligible grids of an idealized and compulsory heterosexuality' (1990: 135), and every other form of sexuality is understood as an imperfect copy of the original and natural heterosexuality. These other sexualities can acquire meaning only in the context of heterosexuality (that is, through the function of heteronormativity). Yet they also demonstrate that not all bodies line up in the normative terms required of them, and Butler argues that all normative performances of gender conceal the ways 'gender discontinuities ... run rampant' (1990: 135) despite the insistence on coherence.

For both Butler and Foucault, Herculine Barbin is clearly an example of a body in which the normativities of gender, sex and desire fail to traverse their proscribed terrain. Yet whereas Barbin presumes his/her ambiguous sex as the cause of his/her desire, Butler argues instead that 'we might read this body ... as a sign of an irresolvable ambivalence produced by the juridical discourse on univocal sex' (1990: 99). The anomaly exists only because of an expectation of singularity, but it is through that anomaly that the limits of that expectation might become apparent. According to Butler, such a reading is at odds with Foucault's. In her discussion of Barbin, Butler highlights the ways in which Foucault idealises Barbin's polymorphous avenues of pleasure, and in the process articulates an emancipatory ideal seemingly at odds with his discussion of sex in the *History of Sexuality*. She argues that in his introduction to Barbin's journals, Foucault 'invokes a trope of prediscursive libidinal multiplicity that effectively presupposes a sexuality "before the law," indeed a sexuality waiting for an emancipation from the shackles of "sex"' (1990: 97). Yet the 'official' Foucault, as Butler describes him, argues that 'sexuality is always situated within matrices of power ... and that recourse to a sexuality before the law is an illusory and complicitous conceit of emancipatory sexual politics' (p. 97).

It is in this latter guise that Butler will utilise Foucault, and it is within that framework that she is particularly interested in Barbin. The 'emancipatory' Foucault, she argues, engages in a commitment to what she describes, in Nietzschean terms, as a 'metaphysics of substance', whereby sex is, in the end, characterised as a 'substantive thing'. Butler also finds the metaphysics of substance in Beauvoir, Wittig and Irigaray, all of whom (despite their commitment to the production of sex) come to articulate some form of sexual difference as something one might be or have. Butler quotes Michel Haar, who argues that according to Nietzsche, 'The subject, the self, the individual, are just so many false concepts, since they transform into substances fictitious unities having at the start only a linguistic reality' (Butler 1990: 21).

Butler's theory of gender performativity, in which gender is a process that must be repeated over the course of a subject's life, and that is reconstituted as new subjects move in and out of being, differentiates her account of the production of sex from the theorists of sex-construction that she both utilises and critiques. For Butler gender is a performance, and a performance is not something one has or something one is, but rather something one does. Because gender is a performance, a culturally sanctioned doing, then the opportunity to undo, or to at least intervene in that doing, must reside in the very means by which gender is produced. The task, as she sees it, is to rethink the 'possibilities for sexuality and identity within the terms of power itself' (1990: 30), rather than seeking to locate resistance outside or prior to heteronormative signifying systems.

It is for this reason that Butler is so interested in the 'unintelligible' bodies that for her demonstrate the very limits of intelligibility, as what they also demonstrate is that the very production of normative sexuality contains the possibility of its resistance. In arriving at this conclusion, Butler draws on Foucault's account of the generative capacities of power, and his critique of what he terms the 'repressive hypothesis'. In the first volume of the *History of Sexuality*, Foucault argues that the Victorian period was characterised by an 'incitement to discourse', rather than the prohibitions on the articulation of sexuality usually associated with that period. Foucault argues that the prevailing contention of a 'power of repression exerted by our society on sex' is inadequate in its failure to account for the series of 'reinforcements and intensifications' (2008: 72) around sex that his genealogical account demonstrates. For Foucault power is productive: he argues that prohibitions work to generate, rather than repress, the discursive effects of desire.

THE TABOO ON INCEST

With a Foucaltian model of power in mind, Butler devotes a significant portion of *Gender Trouble* (the entire second chapter) to one of the most trenchant prohibitions on sexual contact in culture – the taboo on incest. Taking a conception of power as productive, Butler seeks to demonstrate that the incest taboo functions as a heteronormative mechanism that institutes gender identity (1990: x). She does this primarily by rereading Freudian psychoanalysis through Foucault's critique of the repressive hypothesis. Butler's interest in the incest taboo derives largely from the way it is positioned in structural anthropology, and in psychoanalysis, as (respectively) a foundational moment of culture, and of the intelligible subject.

Her analysis of both is framed with a warning that hints at the Foucaltian critique to come. In the second chapter of *Gender Trouble*, Butler notes that feminist theory has, at times, sought to imagine and articulate a time prior to patriarchy (1990: 35). She argues that the universalising ways in which patriarchy tends to be framed in these imaginings risk reifying the very patriarchal structure that feminism opposes. In invoking reification – the mechanism by which the social relations that produce something are disappeared from view – Butler continues the genealogical consideration of history that underpins her text. Thus her concern is that the representation of patriarchy as a repressive and constant singular law risks the elision of the social and cultural contexts in which that law is continually reproduced. The social relations that Butler will argue are most usually elided in such a narrative are the operations of heterosexual hegemony, the 'heterosexual matrix' of this chapter's title. According to Butler, if feminist theory fails to pay critical attention to the ways in which gender positions are produced via the heterosexual matrix, rather than as an over-arching law of repression, then it misreads the structure of power and risks missing the very opportunities to intervene in the production of gender that underpin the feminist project.

Butler begins her discussion of the incest taboo by turning to Lévi-Strauss, whose work influences and inflects that of Lacanian psychoanalysis. In 'The Elementary Structures of Kinship', Lévi-Strauss argues that the taboo on incest (that is, the social law that prohibits sexual contact between close relatives) is the primary structuring law in any society. He outlines how this taboo necessitates the exchange of women between social groupings (families, tribes), and argues that this exchange takes the form of a gift exchange (also common to all societies), the basic form of which is marriage. As Rubin argues, the 'result of a gift of women is more profound than the result of other gift transactions, because the relationship thus established is not just one of reciprocity, but one of kinship' (1975: 173). These resulting structures of kinship, and the complex relations of reciprocity between otherwise unconnected social groups that inaugurate and accompany them, lead Lévi-Strauss to conclude that the application of the incest taboo is the foundational moment of culture. Given that this foundational moment reduces all women to items of exchange, for Lévi-Strauss, culture originates with 'the world historical defeat of women' (Rubin 1975: 176).

Both Butler and Rubin critique this rendering of the relationship between the incest taboo and culture, and seek to demonstrate that Lévi-Strauss fails to account for the relationship between the 'foundation' of culture (a concept, of course, antithetical to the anti-foundational impetus of Butler's work), and the structuring system of compulsory heterosexuality. Given that the incest taboo positions women as objects of desire that are exchanged between men, desire is only ever imagined explicitly in this schema as heterosexual. For Butler this is all the more surprising when one considers how the possibility of a homoerotic unconscious structures this system of exchange (1990: 41). As Rubin argues, the imagining of the taboo on incest in such exclusively heterosexual terms must presuppose a 'prior, less articulate taboo on homosexuality' (1975: 180). Butler contends that Lévi-Strauss never acknowledges the operation of this prior taboo, or examines the ways in which incestuous heterosexuality is 'constituted as the ostensibly natural and pre-artificial matrix of desire' (1990: 42). Instead he insists that incestuous relations between mother and son are a 'pervasive cultural fantasy' (p. 42), a conclusion that serves to reconstitute the heteronormative blind spot in his work.

Both Rubin and Butler question the way in which the law is imagined in the structuralist account of the incest taboo in singular and oppressive terms. Rubin (continuing her conversation with Marxism) describes the exchange of women as 'neither a definition of culture nor a system in and of itself' (1975: 176–7), but as part of a system of production that is dependent upon the economics of the sex/gender system. In short, she rejects Lévi-Strauss's claim that the incest taboo is the foundational moment of culture. Rubin argues instead that the reduction of women to items of exchange does not structure social relations, but is an example of how 'certain relations' transform the biological raw of sex into gender.

Butler's complication of the sex/gender distinction necessitates a different position, and in *Gender Trouble* she rereads 'The Traffic in Women' through the Foucaltian frame that she contends it implies. In particular, Butler points out, Rubin's model of power is a productive one, especially around the issue of sexual identity. Rubin argues that through the incest taboo, gender functions as 'not only an identification with one sex; it also entails that sexual desire is directed toward the other sex' (1975: 180). Both gender identity and sexual identity are constituted through a prohibition on incest that Butler describes as 'primarily productive in its effects' (1990: 73). Whereas Rubin contends that the removal of compulsory heterosexuality would simultaneously remove gender and leave an unmarked sex, Butler argues that such a position falsely imagines an idealised sexuality locatable before the law, and argues that this 'recourse to a happier state' (p. 76) is produced by the very understanding of power (as singular and universal) that Rubin implicitly critiques. Explicitly applying Foucault's critique of the repressive hypothesis, Butler argues that the incest taboo produces both the desire that it prohibits, and the notion of an original sexuality that precedes it (p. 76).

What Butler is particularly interested in is the extent to which this productivity also contains the means of resisting the heteronormativity it instils. The Foucaltian model that she deploys includes the argument that the operation of power is always accompanied by the capacity to, and means of, resisting it. As Foucault puts it, 'there are no relations of power without resistances; the latter are all the more real and effective because they are formed right at the point where relations of power are exercised' (1980b: 142). Butler argues that in its generativity, the incest taboo 'inadvertently produces a variety of substitute desires and identities that are in no sense constrained in advance' (1990: 76) even as it prohibits certain sexual relations. Rereading the incest taboo through Foucault thus enables a consideration of how that taboo might generate the means of resisting the heterosexuality it institutes as the only legitimate framework of desire.

In order to describe the relationship between the incest taboo and compulsory heterosexuality more fully, and to explore the possibility of resistance in Foucaltian terms, Butler turns to the field that has produced perhaps the most influential framework for the constitution of gender – Freudian psychoanalysis. Freud's account of the Oedipal phase of child development provides a detailed analysis of the psychic process by which subjects negotiate the normative expectations of gender that govern familial and social life. It also designates an awareness of a prohibition on maternal incest as a crucial stage in a child's awareness of desire.

According to Freud, in the Oedipus complex normative sexual subjectivity is achieved through the resolution of the child's unconscious incestual desire for its mother. Somewhere between the ages of three and five, the child becomes cognisant of its place in the structure of the family and within the wider structures of gender. This plays out as follows: the child desires the mother but is faced with the futility of that desire on account of either the castrating presence of its rival, the father (for the boy), or the discovery that it does not have a penis and therefore can never have the mother (for the girl). In the case of the boy, the child renounces his love for the mother and identifies with the father. In the case of the girl, the mother is rejected as a love object (partly on account of her corresponding lack of a penis), and the child transfers that desire onto the father. Her ultimate identification with the mother is slightly more complex, as it revolves around an identification with the capacity/desire to bear a child to the father. Nonetheless in either case, the successful resolution of the Oedipal crisis is identification with the same-sex parent, and the inauguration of the child into the structure of heterosexuality.

Butler's interest in Freud's theory of the Oedipal stage is concerned, in particular, with two (related) issues: the taboo on homosexuality, and the relationship between heterosexuality and melancholia. In relation to the first of these, Butler argues (just as Rubin claims of Lévi-Strauss) that the Freudian account of child development presumes, but never articulates, a prior taboo on homosexuality. Freud contends that all children begin as bisexual and direct desire toward both their parents. Yet Freud characterises this bisexuality as the existence of masculine and feminine 'dispositions', and equates a masculine disposition (whatever the gender of the child) as desire for the mother, and a feminine disposition with desire for the father. Bisexuality, as Butler argues, is thus for Freud 'the coincidence of two heterosexual desires within a single psyche' (1990: 61), without any explanation as to why desire cannot be considered in homosexual terms.

In addressing Freud's discounting of the possibility of homosexuality, Butler asks how he comes to distinguish between the dispositions he connects to this heterosexualised bisexuality, and the internalised identifications he associates with normative gender development. In order to describe the implications of what she means by this, Butler turns to Freud's theories on mourning and melancholia. In the essay 'Mourning and Melancholia' (1984), Freud contends that when a subject loses a love-object (for example, in the death of a loved one), the psyche grieves that loss in a state of mourning, but ultimately resolves it by accepting the loss, and investing its libidinal energy in a new love-object (object-cathexis). Melancholia, in contrast, refers to the state of a subject who cannot accept their loss, or, thus, resolve their grief. Instead, unable to let go of the lost object, the psyche seeks to preserve it through incorporating some aspect of it into its own ego. This incorporation of a part of the lost object – a process Freud (1984) terms 'introjection' – thus manifests itself in an identification with the lost love-object rather than a new object-cathexis.

Whereas in this earlier essay Freud characterises melancholia as a pathological state of unresolved mourning, in *The Ego and the Id* (1982) he revises this position. There, as Butler describes it, 'the identification with lost loves characteristic of melancholia becomes the precondition for the work of mourning. The two processes, originally conceived as oppositional, are now understood as integrally related aspects of the grieving process' (1990: 62). Thus, while not all identification is the result of mourning, all states of mourning now include some aspect of identification.

In *Gender Trouble*, and more fully in *The Psychic Life of Power* (1997b), Butler discusses the ramifications of this shift when considered alongside the heteronormativity that underpins the resolution of the Oedipal crisis. She asks whether there might be a way in which 'gender identifications or, rather, the identifications that become central to the formation of gender, are produced through melancholic identification' (1997b: 134–5). Butler's suggestion is that the identification with the same-sex parent that marks the end of the Oedipal crisis, and the corresponding assumption of (hetero)normative gender identity, might in fact be a melancholic identification with the same-sex parent as a lost love object. Because (homosexual) gender identification with the opposite sex is untenable, the masculinity that for the boy is marked by identification with the father is forever 'haunted by the love it cannot grieve' (p. 138). Normative masculinity is marked by a disavowed identification with the feminine that is also the irresolvable grief of homosexual loss.

In *Undoing Gender* (2004) Butler summarises the significance of heterosexual melancholia by explaining that in drawing attention to the relationship between homosexual attachment and the heterosexualised consolidation of gender norms, she is seeking to demonstrate how a prohibition on certain forms of love becomes installed as an ontological truth about the subject: 'The "am" of "I am a man" encodes the prohibition "I may not love a man"' (2004: 199). Thus the truth of gender, or the announcement of sex, always simultaneously cites a prior repudiation of homosexuality. This is the force of prohibition, the repression of a prior truth about that gendered subject (a truth of course that for Butler is as ontologically suspect as the truth that would displace it). Yet if we return to Foucault we can see that because it is the prohibition that produces identification, the 'I may not love a man' is in fact generative of the 'I am a man'. It is the unspoken (and ungrievable) taboo on homosexuality that produces gender identity, rather than the normative resolution of naturalised heterosexual desire. In short, heteronormativity produces gender.

SUBVERSIVE REPETITION

Butler's aim in *Gender Trouble* is to critique the way gender has been understood in feminist theory (as distinct from sex, as unconnected to heteronormativity), and posit an alternative model of gender constitution that takes account of the limits and omissions she identifies. A great deal of Butler's work on gender since the publication of that text has been to revise and revisit its central conceits in response to feminist critique, and to changes in the cultural, social and theoretical field of gender. Certainly, as she herself notes, the connections between heterosexual melancholia and gender performativity are not made particularly clear in *Gender Trouble* (1999: xv).

In *Bodies That Matter* (1993) and *The Psychic Life of Power* (1997b), Butler more explicitly connects melancholic identification with the production, and the troubling, of gender norms. These latter discussions (which we will address in the following chapter) build on the final part of *Gender Trouble*, where Butler begins to work through the ways in which the performative constitution of gender identity might also provide the mechanisms for its subversion.

This subversive potential centres on the need for a performative to repeat in order to continually re-establish its citational legitimacy. As we discussed earlier, Butler argues that the 'appearance of substance' that accrues to the act of gender is dependent upon the repetition of gender performance, a repetition that is 'at once a reenactment and reexperiencing of a set of meanings already socially established' (1990: 140). Performative repetition is a citation that constitutes the repeated fiction as a verifying authority. To describe a child as 'so like a boy', for example, identifies a repeated performance of gender, but simultaneously reaffirms a prior truth of boyness through its very citation of the norm. According to Butler, disrupting the chain of citation by highlighting discontinuities of repetition threatens to reveal that the truth of gender is a regulatory fiction sustained by a 'stylized repetition of acts' (1990: 140) that effect their own legitimating authority. She argues that:

> The possibilities of gender transformation are to be found precisely in the arbitrary relation between such acts, in the possibility of a failure to repeat, a deformity, or a parodic repetition that exposes the phantasmatic effect of abiding identity as a politically tenuous construction. (p. 141)

To that end, Butler highlights the 'cultural practices of drag, cross-dressing, and the sexual stylization of butch/femme lesbian identities' (p. 141) as subjective enactments that might politicise their own failure to repeat properly. She offers up the possibility that, as a consequence, such performances of gender could reveal the fictional naturalisation of gender unity, and its relationship to compulsory heterosexuality.

Butler argues, for example, that drag exercises its subversive potential by complicating the relation between 'imitation' and 'original' in gender performance, repeating gender in such a way as to reveal its reliance on repetition. It is drag's cultural status as a misperformance of gender that foregrounds gender *as* a performance, but also as one that is culturally mandated to cohere with sex. Thus, she argues that:

As much as drag creates a unified picture of 'woman' … it also reveals the distinctness of those aspects of gendered experience which are falsely naturalized as a unity through the regulatory fiction of heterosexual coherence. *In imitating gender, drag implicitly reveals the imitative structure of gender itself – as well as its contingency.* (1990: 137, emphasis in original)

Thus drag can denaturalise, through parody, the claims to authentic gender identities on which heterosexual hegemony depends.

Butler makes similar claims in relation to butch-femme. As we discuss more fully in the next chapter, butch-femme relationships are often targeted in lesbian feminism, where they are condemned in some quarters as an uncritical representation and eroticisation of an oppressive heterosexuality. But Butler argues that such readings tend to leave a hierarchy of sexual identity in place that accords heterosexuality the status of original. In contrast, she asserts that butch-femme can be read not as a copy of this original heterosexuality, but rather as a demonstration of:

how the so-called originals, men and women within the heterosexual frame, are similarly constructed, performatively established. So the ostensible copy is not explained through reference to an origin, but the origin is understood to be as performative as the copy. (2004: 209)

CONCLUSION

The possibilities Butler ascribes to subversive performativity underline the genealogical methodology that frames *Gender Trouble*, and the influence of Foucault in relation to that approach. For Butler, butch-femme or drag are performances that offer the possibility of subverting the appearance of heterosexuality as a sexuality without history, and they do so via the very mechanisms by which that appearance is sustained – that is, through the requirement that gender norms repeat not merely to found a body in the discourse of sex but to authorise its ongoing legitimacy.

As Butler argues in the final chapter of *Bodies That Matter*, the same logic of subversive repetition can be found in the theoretical and activist deployment of 'queer'. For Butler, the homophobic use of the insult 'queer' appears as a self-contained insult, rather than as a repetition of an insult, and this appearance masks the fact that the normative boundaries that it is re-establishing have a history (and it is this history that gives the insult its force). Thus for Butler, the significance of the theoretical appropriation of queer lies not in a strategy to reclaim a homophobic insult in order to deprive it of its capacity to injure. Rather, it is in how the (mis)use of a term that functions performatively lays bare the ways in which performatives function. In the following chapter we examine how Butler theorises that possibility, and the connections and critiques that characterise her relationship to queer theory.

FURTHER READING

Benhabib, S. et al. (1995) *Feminist Contentions*. New York: Routledge.
Derrida, J. (1988) *Limited Inc*. Evanston: Northwestern University Press.
Lloyd, M. (2008) *Judith Butler*. Cambridge: Polity Press.

3 Queer

INTRODUCTION

In an essay in the 1991 collection, *Inside/Out,* Butler takes issue with the notion of 'lesbian' as place from which to theorise. Noting that elsewhere she has argued that 'identity categories tend to be instruments of regulatory regimes' (Butler 1991: 13), Butler acknowledges the political expediency, at times, of appearing 'under the sign of lesbian', but qualifies that in a wish 'to have it permanently unclear what precisely that sign signifies' (p. 14). In *Gender Trouble* (1990), her critique of women as the subject of feminism seeks to move the framework of the debate away from how to ensure the full representation within that category, and toward questions of what gendered structures of power are sustained by the exclusionary mechanisms of the relationship of inside/outside. Here she similarly draws attention to the operations of normativity that constitute signifiers such as lesbian or gay, even when those signs are deployed with anti-homophobic intent.

Butler articulates what she sees as the risks of the 'coming out' discourse that has functioned at the centre of gay politics since the early days of gay liberation. She argues that the 'promise of a transparent revelation of sexuality' (1991: 15), imagined in the celebration of outness, is a fantasy of discursive control and agency that reproduces one aspect of identity as the total subject:

> For it is always finally unclear what is meant by invoking the lesbian-signifier, since its signification is always to some degree out of one's control, but also because its *specificity* can only be demarcated by exclusions that return to disrupt its claim to coherence. What, if anything, can lesbians be said to share? And who will decide this question, and in the name of whom? (p. 15, emphasis in original)

For Butler, the expectation of stability invoked in the discourse of identity is at odds with the 'necessary trouble' (p. 14) that non-heterosexuality might cause heteronormativity, and with the pleasures connected to that instability. Rather than a rearticulation of 'normative definitions offered by other members of the "gay or lesbian community"', Butler argues that that community might make productive use of the historical status of lesbian and gay as 'impossible identities', and utilise 'sites of disruption, error, confusion, and trouble' as the 'very rallying points for a certain resistance to classification and to identity as such' (p. 16). The difficulty, as she sees it, is in enacting this type of performative resistance in a political context in which identity categories have strategic and material value. Thus Butler is left with a question: 'How to use the sign and avow its temporal contingency at once?' (p. 19).

THE POLITICS OF IDENTITY

Butler is speaking here within a wider context of disquiet, among some lesbian and gay activists and theorists, that 'political necessity' within an increasingly conservative lesbian and gay movement had come to rely on a gay or lesbian identity, repeatedly imagined as both self-evident and natural. The gay liberation movement that emerged in the wake of the Stonewall riots in 1969 was a social and political movement committed to the end of 'the homosexual' through a radical transformation of sexual identity that would reveal the 'essentially polymorphous and bisexual' (Altman 1972: 74) nature of human sexuality. Yet by the mid-1970s the more conservative voices in gay liberation 'took up the idea of a gay minority' (Weeks 1985: 198) and attempted to move it away from the margins and into the mainstream, so a carefully represented model of identity became solidified as the defining discourse of lesbian and gay politics.

Precisely who would be included within that framework of identity, however, and what relationships the struggle for rights might bear to other forms of identity and politics, became a source of tension within the movement. In particular race, gender and class became key fissures of dissent. Those dissenting voices argued that through the marginalisation of racial, gendered or class experience, the universal gay subjectivity apparently being rallied around was, in fact, demonstrably white, middle class and male. Amongst lesbians, bitter debates also erupted around the legitimacy of certain sexual and identity practices, and relationships apparently imitative of heterosexual culture were increasingly critiqued. Singled out for particular opprobrium was the culture of butch-femme, which was repeatedly characterised as an unacceptable reproduction of models of 'heteropatriarchy' (Jeffreys 1989: 178), and sadomasochism (SM), which some lesbian feminists condemned for eroticising violence against women.

For Butler and other lesbian and gay theorists, such debates demonstrate that the insistence on the necessity of identity that dominated lesbian and gay politics threatened to install another violence in place of the homophobic violence that this politics sought to erase. Butler poses a series of questions that draw attention to the politics of who or what might instil, and insist upon, the particular frameworks of identity being used:

> Ought such threats of obliteration [of lesbians and gays] dictate the terms of the political resistance to them, and if they do, do such homophobic efforts to that extent win the battle from the start ... Which version of lesbian and gay ought to be rendered visible, and which internal exclusions will that rendering visible institute ... Is it not a sign of despair over public politics when identity becomes its own policy, bringing with it those who 'police' it from various sides? (1991: 19)

As she does in relation to gender, Butler here draws attention to the ways in which adherence to a model of identity replays and reconstitutes the exclusionary mechanisms that underpin oppression. The category of 'lesbian', like that of 'women', is an operation of constraining normativity. The identity-based politics that Butler critiques here is anchored primarily in an essentialised understanding of sexuality. Within the lesbian and gay movement, Diana Fuss argues that:

> The notion of a gay essence is relied upon to mobilize and to legitimate gay activism; 'gay pride', 'gay culture', 'gay sensibility' are all summoned as cornerstones of the gay community, indices of the emergence of a long-repressed collective identity. (1989: 97)

Thus essentialists (and Fuss simultaneously critiques the universalising problematic of the term) located a universal homosexual desire (repressed) across history, and mobilised it as a uniting political force. Just as essentialist/

constructionist debates were waged in feminism, similar discussions occurred among lesbian and gay scholars, and the essentialist model was increasingly displaced by an analysis of how meaning had been constructed in relation to same-sex desire throughout (primarily Western) history. This 'constructionist' critique utilised historical accounts of the social meanings of desire, and argued that same-sex sexual (and emotional) relationships across history were not necessarily connected to any form of sexual identity.

The work of Foucault is particularly influential in such accounts. As discussed in the previous chapter, in *The History of Sexuality* (2008) Foucault traces the development of sexual identity as an effect of discursive networks of power. He challenges dominant understandings of the Victorian period as repressive, and argues instead that a quantitative increase in discourses of perversity, and the largely confessional form those discourses took, contributed to an understanding of perversity as occupying particular embodied spaces. As this discourse developed, a new 'specification of individuals' became intimately linked with the perversions in which those individuals engaged:

> Homosexuality appeared as one of the forms of sexuality when it was transposed from the practice of sodomy onto a kind of interior androgyny, a hermaphrodism of the soul. The sodomite had been a temporary aberration; the homosexual was now a species. (2008: 43)

Accounts such as Foucault's (along with Jeffrey Weeks, who also identified the solidification of homosexual desire into gay identity) came to occupy positions of critical importance in lesbian and gay scholarship, particularly when combined with the growing influence of post-structuralism. Rather than the unified bounded subject imagined in identity-based politics, post-structuralism theorises subjectivity as 'a site of disunity and conflict' (Weedon 1987: 21); and any identity emanating from, or attached to, that subject, is therefore recast as a 'sustaining and persistent cultural fantasy' (Jagose 1996: 78). Given that in post-structural accounts 'there is no true self that exists prior to its immersion in culture' (Sullivan 2003: 41), it follows that there can be no inner truth – no essence – to gay subjectivity. Not only is homosexuality constituted through discourse (as Weeks and Foucault argue), but discursive regimes produce the fictions of stability and universality that mask those processes of constitution.

QUEER THEORY

Since Theresa de Lauretis's widely credited first use of the term 'queer theory' (de Lauretis 1991) to mark a critical distance from lesbian and gay studies, queerness has functioned, in part, as a critique of the politics of identity that underpins the (arguably) more normative accounts of lesbian and gay. According to David Halperin, the usefulness of queer is dependent upon resisting the reification of queer as a definitive thing, and reproducing it instead as an ongoing project of resistance (1995: 66). Thus, he suggests that there is 'nothing in particular' to which queer 'necessarily refers' (p. 62), because queer seeks to disrupt the determinacy that normatively marks identity. That there is nothing *in particular* to which queer *necessarily* refers denotes a generalised anti-normativity as the field of queer, but also positions queer as in excess, but never independent, of the gender imperatives of heteronormativity. As Annamarie Jagose notes, queer does not exist 'outside the magnetic field of identity' (1996: 132). In fact, the field of identity is precisely the performative terrain on which queerness is to be most usefully enacted. In Butler's account, queer interventions in gender performativity fix on and cite the imperatives of identity, and reveal the limits of their repeatability through what Butler identifies as 'hyperbolic mimicry' (1993: 232). While there is no uniformity in what queer refers to, queer nonetheless must refer; and that referral is, in fact, its primary strategy.

Eve Sedgwick describes an evocative moment of signification that reveals precisely how queer at once utilises and disturbs nominally coherent productions of sexual identity:

At the 1992 gay pride parade in New York City, there was a handsome, intensely muscular man in full leather regalia, sporting on his distended chest a T-shirt that read KEEP YOUR LAWS OFF MY UTERUS. The two popular READ MY LIPS T-shirts marketed by ACT UP were also in evidence, and by the thousands. But for the first time it was largely gay men who were wearing the version of the shirt that features two turn-of-the-century-looking women in a passionate clinch. Most of the people wearing the version with the osculating male sailors, on the other hand, were lesbians. FAGGOT and BIG FAG were the T-shirt legends self-applied by many, many women; DYKE and the more topical LICK BUSH by many, many men ... And everywhere at the march, on women and on men, there were T-shirts that said simply: QUEER. It was a QUEER time. (1993: xi)

The wearing of a T-shirt that announces one's sexuality is a performative act of outing that simultaneously performs sexual identity. The queer performance that Sedgwick describes in the shifting and swapping of signifiers still functions performatively, and still utilises the same strategies of identification, but it does so in order to effect a deliberate discordance with normative expectations.

This utilisation of the signs of sexual identity against themselves produces precisely the semiotic confusion most commonly imagined as definitive of queer and of its indeterminacy. What is of particular importance in these repetitions of identity performance that fail (that is, do not perform that repetition properly) is the extent to which, in order to engage confusion, the refusal must utilise the tools of recognition in order to disturb their recognisability. As Butler insists, the operations that might disturb the field of power can be found at the very points at which power is exercised, and not from some fantasy of an outside position or space. Thus, her theorisation of gender performativity includes an ongoing insistence that to escape the categories of identity by which bodies are made legible is a cultural fantasy underwritten by heteronormativity. In *Bodies That Matter*, Butler cites Derrida to emphasise the contexts of referral that sustain the power of performative force: 'Could a performative succeed ... if its formulation did not repeat a "coded" or iterable utterance ... if it were not identifiable in some way as a "citation"?' (Derrida 1982: 18). Iterability is critical to the practices of queer: the T-shirt wearers repeat the announcement of gayness in order to produce it as queerness.

It is in this commitment to 'rethinking the subjective meaning of sexuality' that Michael Warner locates queer's potential contribution to 'new ways of thinking through the persistence of heteronormativity in social ideologies and institutions' (1993: x–xi). Heteronormativity, defined by Warner as 'heterosexual culture's exclusive ability to interpret itself as society' (p. xxi), is a key target of critique, and a site of intervention. Because normativity in general is the network of power in which the performativities of gender and sexuality function as disciplining forces, anti-normativity in general thus becomes the field of queer. Queerness is 'by definition *whatever* is at odds with the normal, the legitimate, the dominant' (Halperin 1995: 62), and this includes the ways in which gay or lesbian identity, or the aims of lesbian and gay politics, are policed according to normative parameters.

This final point is an important one. The capacity of anti-homophobic politics to utilise and reaffirm the regulatory mechanisms that privilege some bodies over others persists among the dominant voices of mainstream lesbian and gay politics. In *Undoing Gender*, Butler refers to this through the example of gay marriage. She argues that:

> The recent efforts to promote lesbian and gay marriage also promote a norm that threatens to render illegitimate and abject those sexual arrangements that do not comply with the marriage norm in either its existing or revisable form. (2004: 5)

For Michael Warner (and, it is safe to assume, for Butler) the arguments repeatedly mobilised in the gay marriage campaign offer the promise to a heteronormative and homophobic society that:

> Marriage, in short, would make for good gays – the kind who would not challenge the norms of straight culture, who would not flaunt sexuality, and who would not insist on living differently from ordinary folk. (1999: 113)

The censoring replication of heteronorms that both Butler and Warner contend the gay marriage campaign can effect was played out precisely following a performance by openly gay *American Idol* runner-up Adam Lambert at the 2009 American Music Awards. That performance featured Lambert leading a dancer around on a leash, 'getting his privates grabbed by a tutu-wearing female dancer' and 'forcefully' kissing his male keyboard player (Everett 2009). Within the inevitable media discussion that followed was an article by Jennifer Vanasco (2009) in *The Huffington Post*, entitled 'How Adam Lambert is Hurting Gay Marriage'. Within it, Vanasco chastises Lambert for the thoughtlessness of a performance that offered up to mainstream America precisely what it fears most about gays. Vanasco argues that:

> This is why mainstream America votes against gays, Adam Lambert. Not because of people who have families and jobs and bills and weddings. Because of people like you, who use sexuality thoughtlessly in order to advance your own agenda.

Vanasco's criticism of Lambert enacts precisely the heteronormative censorship that both Butler and Warner describe – only some performances of gayness are to be sanctioned within a narrowly defined 'gay cause', and those performances are the ones that do not threaten the 'civil rights', as Vanasco puts it, of those gays and lesbians wanting acceptability in the mainstream. Nowhere does Vanasco question why 'mainstream America' gets to decide what is and isn't acceptable with regard to manifestations of desire, and in (not) doing so, she replicates the very structures of recognition that, according to Butler, will always and only privilege heterosexuality.

Queer politics and theory seek to trace and produce those moments in which the categories of identity, and the normative politics often deployed in their name, cannot contain the possibilities of what bodies can do. Butler argues that when:

> The disorganization and disaggregation of the field of bodies disrupt the regulatory fiction of heterosexual coherence ... that regulatory ideal is exposed as a norm and a fiction that disguises itself as a developmental law regulating the sexual field that it purports to describe. (1990: 136)

Within this logic the technologies of power that regulate the hegemonic field of sexual identification are exposed by those bodies that fail to map according to those norms of identity. Bodies subvert those norms by using sexual identification against itself in a way that opens it up to new, permanently contingent, possibilities.

As Sedgwick describes it, queer can refer to:

> the open mesh of possibilities, gaps, overlaps, dissonances and resonances, lapses and excesses of meaning when the constituent elements of anyone's gender, of anyone's sexuality aren't made (or *can't* be made) to signify monolithically. (1993: 8, emphasis in original)

It is not difficult to see why Butler's work is so central to the development of queer theory. According to Butler, the fictions of gender truth are sustained by a heteronormative insistence on their ongoing (re)production. Given that gender is as much a discursive construct as the binarised hetero/homosexuality, Butler argues that the ostensible and ongoing maintenance of disjunctions between culturally constituted, and natural, dimensions of maleness and femaleness (such as that posited in the sex/gender distinction of some feminist theory) also enables the ongoing privileging of heterosexuality. Heteronormativity and gender legibility both draw on naturalised processes of constitution. The politics of distinctions between what is represented, and what is real, in relation to gender and sexual identity must therefore instead become a politics of how the distinctions between representation and reality are sustained. Following Foucault, Butler employs a genealogical critique that investigates 'the political stakes in designating as an *origin* and *cause* those identity categories that are in fact the *effects* of institutions, practices, discourses' (1990: ix); and insists that it is via discursive performativity that gender identity is constituted. She argues repeatedly that the social, cultural and political categorisations that constitute sexuality do so by privileging heterosexuality, and insists on the limited political utility of any representation of sexuality as identity.

Queer theory is an account of how heterosexual hegemony is sustained in the structures of sexuality, and Butler's theory of performativity is a detailed and sustained account of this regenerative process. Queer politics is often imagined as the utilising of categories of identity in ways that draw attention to the naturalisations of constitutive power that structure and produce sexual subjectivity. Such 'queer performances' often seek to disrupt the repetition of normativity in ways similar to the critical potential to which Butler accords drag and other repetitions that might mimic the structure of gender. Less well elaborated in accounts of queer, yet critical to the disruption that such accounts outline, is Butler's insistence on the disavowed relationship of hetero/homo that structures heterosexuality. According to Butler, in the melancholic structure of heterosexuality, that heterosexuality is always marked by its identification with that which it nominally excludes. The mechanisms of identity that Butler describes demonstrate the ways in which such identifications are rendered opaque.

IDENTIFICATION AND DISAVOWAL

In the introduction to *Inside/Out* (1991), Diana Fuss utilises the figure of inside/outside to interrogate the structuring identification of sexual orientation, and suggests that the border maintaining inside/out may be far more permeable than its binary utilisation allows. Other binaries thus structured by the same separating mechanisms, and undone by the same inabilities of sustaining such separation, may therefore be equally open to transgressions of the oppositional logic they otherwise enact. Homosexuality/heterosexuality, Fuss contends, is just such a binary:

> Thus, homo in relation to the hetero ... operates as an indispensable interior exclusion – an outside which is inside interiority making the articulation of the latter possible, a transgression of the border which is necessary to constitute the border as such. (1991: 3)

A binarised homosexuality is always already constituted in relation to the heterosexuality that marks it as difference. And, as Butler demonstrates in her account of the melancholic structure of heterosexuality, the reverse is simultaneously true. Like Butler, Fuss is far less interested in asking where identity comes from, than she is in asking what work identity categories do in sustaining the very frameworks of oppression under question. Butler and Fuss are examples of lesbian and gay theorists turning their analysis toward how categories of identity are formed into mutually sustaining binary systems that conceal the constitutive relations of difference within identity categories. It is in examining the extent to which such functions of power are naturalised in the knowledges that produce and sustain sexuality as identity, that these queer theories seek to open up new possibilities of resistance by articulating the contingency of demarcations of sexual identity.

In the final chapter of *Bodies That Matter*, in an essay entitled 'Critically Queer', Butler engages with the politicised reappropriation of the term 'queer'. For Butler, the significance of this discursive reversal is connected, in part, to the constitutive power that the insult queer has historically had. Butler characterises this pejorative use of queer as performative, arguing that the queer subject is produced through the 'shaming interpellation' of the taunt of 'queer!' (1993: 226) that is consequent of the force of authority that has accrued to the term in its homophobic use over time. The 'straight world has always needed the queers it has sought to repudiate' (p. 223), because those queers are the visible limits of normalisation, and recognising and announcing a move beyond those limits is a means for the subject who is using the taunt 'queer' to reconstitute and reaffirm their own legitimacy. According to Butler, the extent to which this operates as a performative is dependent upon the historical network which every insult of queer invariably cites. The mechanisms of repetition and citation are crucial to Butler's account of performativity, in part because the everydayness of those mechanisms is so difficult to see. Performatives work because the force of authority accumulates through its very repetition, and in that repetition the performative *'draws on and covers over* the constitutive conventions by which it is mobilized' (p. 227, emphasis in original).

The shared discursive space of the insulter and the insulted leaves the trace of melancholic identification that Butler argues is the constitutive disavowal that structures heteronormativity. In 'Multiculturalism, or the Cultural Logic of Multinational Capitalism', Slavoj Žižek offers a useful example of precisely how this works. Seeking a compelling answer to what he describes as the 'naïve but nonetheless crucial question: why does the Army so strongly resist publicly accepting gays into its ranks?', Žižek asserts that 'there is only one possible consistent answer: because the Army community itself relies on a thwarted/disavowed homosexuality as the key component of the soldiers' male-bonding' (1997: 32). He then describes the excessive permeation of the otherwise extremely homophobic Yugoslav People's Army with an atmosphere of homosexual innuendo. That both the signifiers of homophobia *and of homosexuality* inhabit the same space is not, according to Žižek, merely a quirk of coincidence or an issue of tolerance. Rather, he suggests, the former enables the latter to retain its key role, while not being signified as homosexuality.

Žižek's discussion here is in support of his assertion that a theory of power must account for the way censorship in fact enables 'the marginal or subversive force that the power discourse endeavours to dominate ... to split from within the power discourse itself' (p. 32). Censorship of homosexuality endeavours to (but ultimately cannot) contain and mask the constitutive relationship of that homosexuality to the climate of heterosexuality being established. In the army context Žižek describes (a situation which is, of course, by no means peculiar to the army of the former Yugoslavia) the male bonding that a successful army requires functions as both the source, and the effect, of power. In an example Žižek uses, in which soldiers greet each other with the demand to 'smoke my prick' (pp. 32–3), the homophobic utterance functions as an imperative for the requester and the requestee to inhabit the same abjected space. The insult positions homosexuality as the most demeaned of subjectivities, but simultaneously acknowledges that this humiliation is dependent upon the insulter participating in the activities imagined as so definitive of that subjection. It plays out an aggressive repudiation of homosexuality that is, at the same time, an identification.

Žižek's discussion has clear resonances with the repudiation of homosexuality that Butler argues structures heterosexual identification. In *The Psychic Life of Power*, she also discusses the disavowal that underpins the prohibition on gays in the military:

And it is, we might conjecture, precisely the fear of setting homosexuality loose from this circuit of renunciation that so terrifies the guardians of masculinity in the U.S. military. What would masculinity 'be' without this aggressive circuit of renunciation from which it is wrought? Gays in the military threaten to undo masculinity only because this masculinity is made of repudiated homosexuality. (1997b: 143, emphasis in original)

For Butler, moments at which the mutual dependence of hetero and homo is revealed (in whatever capacity) simultaneously reveal a crisis at the heart of a heterosexuality established through performativity. In the process that she describes in *Bodies That Matter*, an abjected homosexuality is relegated to the imaginary precisely because of its constitutive relation to heterosexuality, and to the terms by which heterosexuality gets to function as normativity. For Butler, what this suggests (and what is immediately disavowed) is the risk that there is a 'possible identification *with* an abject homosexuality at the heart of heterosexual identification' (1993: 111). As she makes clear:

a radical refusal to identify with a given position suggests that on some level an identification has already taken place, an identification that is made and disavowed, a disavowed identification whose symptomatic appearance is the insistence on, the overdetermination of, the identification by which gay and lesbian subjects come to signify in public discourse. (p. 113)

Thus despite its relegation to the imaginary, the prohibited possibility of homosexuality is always implicit in the heterosexual frame, haunting the borders of the body. Discursive performativity thus fails 'to finally and fully establish the identity to which it refers' (p. 188), and this failure troubles the political terms that are meant to establish a coherent identity. In the homophobic performance that taunts 'queer', or delineates it by momentarily taking up that abjected space, is the anxiety marking all performative repetition: will the relationship of constitution continue to be covered over even as it is drawn upon?

In *Epistemology of the Closet* (1990) (the text that, alongside *Gender Trouble*, is routinely cited as foundational to the field of queer theory) Eve Sedgwick identifies the same disavowal of the constitutive relationship between homo and hetero, and argues that the opportunities for resignification made available in the moments of contradiction are not necessarily the preserve of destabilising initiatives. Sedgwick sets out an examination of how the relationship between heterosexuality and homosexuality is constructed via particular operations of knowledges, ignorances and spaces of contradiction. The silences and ignorance in particular that circulate around what she describes as the 'chronic, now endemic crisis of homo/heterosexual definition' (1990: 1) routinely produce definitional contradictions.

Using a deconstructive approach, Sedgwick demonstrates that heterosexuality both requires and repudiates homosexuality in order to sustain its normative status. This apparently contradictory relationship of dependence and subjugation produces particular definitional instabilities. Sedgwick argues that despite the presentation of homosexual and heterosexual as symmetrical binary oppositions, their relationship is a more dynamic and unsettled one:

> first, term B is not symmetrical with but subordinated to term A; but, second, the ontologically valorized term A actually depends for its meaning on the simultaneous subsumption and exclusion of term B; hence, third, the question of priority between the supposed central and supposed marginal category of each dyad is irresolvably unstable, an instability caused by the fact that term B is constituted as at once internal and external to term A. (1990: 10)

What her analysis demonstrates is that this crisis of homo/hetero definition – a crisis we might also understand as the recognisable threat that the *lack* of distinction of desire between gay and straight might emerge fully into the social consciousness – produces and sustains cultural representations of the relationships between gay and straight. Where that line is clearly blurred is also where it must be most rigorously controlled, which is precisely the point made by Žižek and Butler. Sexual identity (as homosexuality), and the 'disclosure' of it, is enacted as a naturalised representation of what is, in fact, a fiction of definition. Whether pursued in the service of homophobic or anti-homophobic ends, sexual differentiation is channelled through an organising binary that must anxiously and repeatedly reassert its own existence.

Locating and understanding this irresolvable instability, as Sedgwick makes clear, is not in and of itself transformative. Acknowledgement of the permeability of homo/hetero, according to Sedgwick, has always been available, and has 'continually lent discursive authority, to antigay as well as gay cultural forces' (p. 10). Thus, rather than an 'idealist faith' in the 'self-corrosive efficacy of the contradictions' (p. 11) that structure sexual identity, Sedgwick argues that the meanings and deployments of such contradictions are the site at which discursive intervention as antihomophobic strategy can (and should) take place:

> I will suggest instead that contests for discursive power can be specified as competitions for the material and rhetorical leverage required to set the terms of, and to profit in some way from, the operations of such an incoherence of definition. (1990: 11)

THE PROBLEM OF CONTEXT

The importance Sedgwick places on the management of contradiction points to the difficulty for queer, or indeed for any parodic politics, in ensuring that the trouble they perform is read and functions as such. Critical responses to Sacha Baron Cohen's recent film *Bruno* neatly demonstrate the dilemma. In a review in *The Guardian*, Peter Bradshaw (2009) describes how *Bruno* was criticised initially as homophobic, but characterises that criticism as 'the prelude to a lavish celebration for having confronted homophobia', and describes the film as 'unimpeachably progressive'. Other critics are not so sure that the film ever escapes that first reading. Wrapping his critique in the politics of the British class system, Nirpal Dhaliwal (2009) (also of *The Guardian*) sees *Bruno* as evidence that Baron Cohen has a profound (middle-class) discomfort with the idea of men having sex, and that this is 'manifested in his wildly enthusiastic mimickry and ridicule of homosexuality'. The point of this example is not to adjudicate on either position, but rather to demonstrate the difficulty of doing so because of the impossibility of knowing how discursive intervention might be read, or whether indeed it is even intended to disturb.

Similar problems circulate around the deployment of 'camp', the tradition of artifice and irony long associated with the performance of gayness. Richard Dyer, for example, argues that the 'ironic stance' that camp takes up has been deliberately utilised to 'denaturalise' the constructions of gender:

> Far from expressing a sense of what is natural, it constantly draws attention to the artifices attendant on the construction of images of what is natural. Camp, drag and macho self-consciously play the signs of gender, and it is in the play and exaggeration that an alternative sexuality is implied – a sexuality, that is, that recognizes itself as in a problematic relationship to the conventional conflation of sexuality and gender. (2002: 40)

In an article in the *New Statesman*, which pays particular attention to the gayness of the makeover experts that increasingly populate reality television, John Lyttle connects the artifice of the historical context of television camp to a 'politics and purpose' that function as an 'essentially subversive' opportunity to get 'you heterosexuals to swallow something you really, *really* didn't want to put in your mouths' (2004: 29, emphasis in original). According to Lyttle, this is the camp of such performers as John Inman, Frankie Howerd, Kenneth Williams, Danny La Rue and Kenny Everett, and continues through contemporary figures such as Lily Savage, Julian Clary and Graham Norton. Lyttle distinguishes such politicised campness by affording it a capital 'C'. 'Lower-case camp', in contrast, functions almost solely as a 'light entertainment phenomenon' (p. 28), and offers a formulaic paradigm in which '[d]espite three decades of diversity, it appears that gay men are still best suited to be a) grooming gurus, b) fashion savants, c) food and wine connoisseurs, d) design doctors or e) culture vultures' (p. 29). This is precisely (and deliberately) the paradigm offered by the recent makeover show *Queer Eye for the Straight Guy*.

In both the theorisation of resistance, and in the critique of its efficacy, there are clear resonances here with Butler's use of drag in her discussion of gender performativity. Butler argues that representations which disrupt and reveal the naturalisation of gender identity are potentially transformative. In both camp and drag, the subversiveness of hyperbolic enactments is precisely in their excessive acquiescence to gender normativities, and thus there is an excessive effeminacy to the archetypal camp gay man. Cementing the connection between the politics of drag and the politics of camp is Moe Meyer's assertion that Camp (deliberately denoted with a capital 'C') is '*solely* a queer ... discourse' that embodies a 'specifically queer cultural critique' (1994: 1, emphasis in original). According to Meyer, any version of camp not originating in a context of queer is an appropriating derivative rather than a different kind of Camp. Camp is always parodic, always political, and always productive of queer.

In the claims and confusions around camp/Camp, drag and queer, are the shared problematics of distinguishing between performances that disturb, and those that repeat and reconfirm, performatives of gender and sexuality. Kleinhaus argues 'that it defines itself in difference from the dominant culture does not automatically construct Camp as radically oppositional' (Meyer 1994: 195). The line between irony and stereotype (and the moment at which camp becomes stereotype, and vice versa) is by no means clearly delineated, uniform across contexts, or guaranteed to always be read as such.

Like Sedgwick and Kleinhaus, Butler is aware of the capacity of heteronormative culture to withstand (even to engender) the performance that draws attention to its array of contradictions. She cautions against imagining a destabilising politics in all parody, and in a key passage argues that:

> Parody by itself is not subversive, and there must be a way to understand what makes certain kinds of parodic repetitions effectively disruptive, truly troubling, and which repetitions become domesticated and rearticulated as instruments of cultural hegemony. (1990: 139)

Yet Butler gives no indication of what that 'way to understand' might be, and dismisses a 'typology of actions' (p. 139) that would take little account of context. Indeed, in a 1992 interview she notes that 'there is no easy way to know whether something is subversive', and that what she means by subversion 'are those effects that are incalculable' (Kotz 1992: 84). In the same discussion, she concedes that her use of drag in *Gender Trouble* may have been a mistake 'because many people have now understood that to be the *paradigm* for performativity, and that's not the case' (p. 84, emphasis in original). Certainly, Butler's subsequent discussions of drag are often marked by her assertion that drag is not in and of itself necessarily political, and that she never intended drag to function as the exemplary performance that would disturb the operation of normativity. What Butler argues is that 'for a copy to be subversive of heterosexual hegemony it has to both mime and displace its conventions. And not all miming is displacing' (p. 84). In fact she points to an example of drag that she uses in *Bodies That Matter*, the film *Paris is Burning*, as an example of miming that 'actually reinvests the gender ideals … reconsolidates their hegemonic status' (p. 84). Despite her subsequent misgivings about 'a text I probably wrote too quickly', Butler maintains that a performance of drag can contain or occasion 'a certain implicit theorization of gender' that demonstrates 'what can only be called the transferability of the [gender] attribute' (2004: 213).

Nonetheless, critics of Butler argue that her theory of performativity, and in particular her account of drag, fail to fully account for the social and material contexts in which gender is (or cannot be) misperformed. In a critique informed by Marxism, Rosemary Hennessy, for example, argues that the materialism that Butler utilises is unable to account for links between discursive practices of resignification, and the social and economic conditions that make such performances possible (2000: 117). According to Hennessy, the 'version of materialism' proffered by Butler, particularly in *Bodies That Matter*, is a materiality understood as 'simply a matter of norms' (p. 55). In Butler's account of performativity, norms materialise sex through reiteration and citation. Hennessy suggests that Butler's connection of normative heterosexuality to the social makes a useful contribution to the post-structuralist account of identity in its utilisation of some measure of 'social and historical analysis' (pp. 56–7). Nonetheless, she contends that 'understanding the materiality of social life as so exclusively normative also limits social relations to the domains of culture and the law' (p. 57). Thus, the dimensions of social life outside of the regulation of normative discourse that Butler establishes are excluded from her account. According to Hennessy, the materialisation of the body is thus a body understood outside the determining forces of capital.

In demonstrating what this might mean, Hennessy examines Butler's use of drag as a type of gender misperformance not always accessible in a social context characterised by economic inequity, and thus raises the question of who, or what, has the capacity to attach meaning to those moments that might be queer? While Butler acknowledges that the meaning of gender troubling is dependent on 'a context and reception in which subversive confusions can be fostered' (1990: 139), Hennessy argues that Butler fails to answer the crucial question of 'what exactly is meant by context here?' (2000: 117).

Hennessy contends that Butler's consideration of the historical fails to historicise; that is, she does not link drag as discursive practice to 'the social relations that make it possible' (p. 117). Moreover, her assumption that '*anyone* might participate in exposing the fiction of sexual identity' (pp. 117–18, emphasis in original) is also disputed by Hennessy. She argues that Butler's assignation of indeterminacy to the signifiers 'lesbian' and 'gay' is not reflected in a social context that insists on such terminologies referring to authentic identities. Hennessy appears here to misread Butler in her claim that they are assigned this by Butler, when, in fact, Butler argues that it is the very 'determinacy' of gender under heterosexual hegemony that informs their utility for queer performance. Nonetheless, Hennessy argues that for those gays and lesbians:

> who have not had the social resources or mobility to insulate themselves from heteronormativity's insistence that sex equals gender, drag has not been so much playful subversion as a painful yearning for authenticity, occasionally with brutally violent results. (p. 118)

So while gender performances that are recognisable failures may indeed, as Butler asserts, fail to fully establish gender normativities, the break they visibly offer in the heteronormative organisational schema may also serve to reaffirm, rather than to disturb, the necessity or inevitability of the compulsory practice of gendering. The body or the performance of the body that looks wrong may thus serve only to re-establish that the body *is* wrong, rather than to provoke critique of the forcible performance of coherent gender identities. Hennessy's critique is one of a number that points to the domain of the material (understood here in Marxist terms as the real conditions of existence experienced in relation to the inequities of class) in order to demonstrate the gulf between queer theory's advocating of a politics of representation, and actual lasting change in the daily experience of most queer bodies (see also Kirsch 2000; Morton 1995). According to the materialist critique, the failure to consider possibilities outside the realm of the cultural limits queer theory's account of how sexual normativity functions.

Butler's work on gender, particularly following *Gender Trouble,* is marked by an insistence on the real effects on bodies of the normative operations of power she describes. In the essay 'Merely Cultural', however, Butler questions the division between social and material reproduction (of gender norms), and the cultural terrain of queer:

> Is it only a matter of 'cultural' recognition when non-normative sexualities are marginalized and debased, or does the possibility of a livelihood come into play? And is it possible to distinguish, even analytically, between a lack of cultural recognition and material oppression, when the very definition of legal 'personhood' is rigorously circumscribed by cultural norms that are indissociable from their material effects? (1997c: 273)

Butler contends that the politics of queer might thus centre on methodological concerns as material effect. She argues that the aim of *Gender Trouble* was to:

> open up the field of possibility for gender without dictating which kinds of possibilities ought to be realized. One might wonder what use 'opening up possibilities'

finally is, but no one who has understood what it is to live in the social world as what is 'impossible,' illegible, unrealizable, unreal and illegitimate is likely to pose that question. (1999: viii)

While such a conclusion threatens to enact its own universalising narrative of experience, Butler's key point here is that the imperative to know in advance what can be precluded as material and political effect inevitably performs the assumption that all that can be (or should be) made legible is already present in discourse.

Critical responses to the possibilities of subversive repetition (both positive and negative) that Butler outlines in *Gender Trouble* have tended to focus almost exclusively on her use of drag. Because of drag's association with hyperbolic and deliberate performance, Butler's utilisation of it to demonstrate the performativity of gender was repeatedly misread as denoting some degree of choice in the taking on of gender attributes, a misreading that often led to the voluntarist 'bad reading' of *Gender Trouble* that we discussed in the previous chapter. In addition (and partly because of feminist concerns that performances of drag also replayed and reconstituted histories of misogyny), some feminists argued that in valorising drag (a contention that she would emphatically dispute), Butler trivialises the material effects of women's experience.

In what William Turner describes as 'a succinct and accessible catalog of the complaints that various critics have lodged against Butler' (2000: 6), Martha C. Nussbaum argues that Butler deploys an inaccessible and apolitical field of parodic play in the absence of any real engagement with the reality of women's material lives, or the actual political work that characterises feminism. In particular, she critiques Butler's use of drag and her insistence on the relationships between discourse and the material. Nussbaum reads Butler as advocating that marginalised subjects are 'doomed to repetition of the power structures into which we are born, but we can at least make fun of them; and some ways of making fun are subversive assaults on the original norms' (1999: 40). What she finds in Butler is a politics that is a non-politics, a 'quietism and retreat' (p. 38) that takes no real account of the material violence done to women via the imperatives of gender. Instead, 'sexy acts of parodic inversion' are proffered in place of 'lasting material or institutional change' (p. 43).

It is in response to this kind of critique that Butler will later insist that the writing of *Gender Trouble* 'was not done simply out of a desire to play with language or prescribe theatrical antics in the place of "real" politics ... It was done from a desire to live, to make life possible, and to rethink the possible as such' (1999: xx). *Bodies That Matter* frames 'the material' as connected to how discourse produces 'the more and the less "human," the inhuman, the humanly unthinkable' (1993: 8). Indeed, it is precisely for these reasons that Butler strengthens, and more fully elaborates, the connections between performativity and melancholia. She points to the AIDS crisis, and the difficulty of:

> finding a public occasion and language in which to grieve this seemingly endless number of deaths as an example of how the impossibility of articulating and resolving homosexual loss manifests itself with very real consequences for very real bodies. (1997b: 138)

Despite the misgivings that Butler has about the ways in which her use of drag has been taken up, it is because of (rather than in spite of) this connection to material life that she continues to utilise it in her discussions of the forcible citation of norms. Thus, she chooses to examine *Paris is Burning* irrespective of what she describes as the 'idealization' of gender norms that its performances of drag, at times, undertake because she sees the text as an example that demonstrates the:

> strong ritual bonds ... which make us aware of the resignification of social bonds that gender minorities within communities of color can and do forge. Thus, we are talking about a cultural life of fantasy that not only organizes the material conditions of life, but which also produces sustaining bonds of community where recognition becomes possible. (2004: 216)

In *Bodies That Matter* she also insists on the politicisation of hyperbolic theatricality discernible in the histories of queer, and cites 'traditions of cross-dressing, drag balls, street walking, butch-femme spectacles ... die-ins by ACT UP; kiss-ins by Queer Nation; drag performance benefits for AIDS' (1993: 232–3) as examples. Butler thus locates within queer a necessary insistence on performing what the materialisation of sex disavows. The '"unliveable" and "uninhabitable" zones of social life which are nevertheless densely populated', and whose population is required (but not acknowledged) to 'circumscribe the domain of the [legitimated] subject' (1993: 8) and perform their own abjection as spectacle. Queerness re-presents the relegation of 'abject beings' to the domain of the outside of intelligible cultures of subjectivity, by repositioning them centre-stage, and insisting on that reappearance as a politics.

Indeed, as Butler demonstrates, the relationship between performativity and melancholia contains the persistent threat that it is in the performance of queer that the extent to which normative heterosexuality is the most fully rendered site of the unliveable will be revealed. In *Bodies That Matter*, Butler pays greater attention (than is the case in *Gender Trouble*) to the psychic dimension of drag; and citing the 'iconographic figure of the melancholic drag queen' (1993: 234) she revisits the relationship between drag and melancholia. Butler argues that drag 'allegorizes' the ungrievable loss that characterises melancholia, and 'thus allegorizes *heterosexual melancholy*' (p. 234, emphasis in original) by performing not the love-object that one cannot be but rather the object that one cannot have. But here, as opposed to the common misconception that posits any performance of drag as a homosexual identification, Butler argues that any gender performance enacts that allegory. Thus, as she puts it, 'The "truest" lesbian melancholic is the strictly straight woman, and the "truest" gay male melancholic is the strictly straight man' (p. 235), because their performance of identification with the object they cannot have is, by far, the most convincing. The performer in drag, in contrast, performs with the awareness that the pleasure of such a performance is that they will always fail to fully approximate the identification they perform.

INDETERMINACY AND COMMODITY CULTURE

Yet it is around the issue of drag that the Marxist critique by theorists such as Hennessey draws attention to the absence, in Butler's work, of any sustained consideration of capitalism as part of the context in which gender trouble might be wrought. Butler briefly takes up the implications of the commodity culture on which capitalism depends when she revisits the model of subversion outlined in *Gender Trouble*, ten years after its publication:

Just as metaphors lose their metaphoricity as they congeal through time into concepts, so subversive performances always run the risk of becoming deadening clichés through their repetition and, most importantly, through their repetition within commodity culture where 'subversion' carries market value. (1999: xxi)

Given the relative proliferation of representations of lesbians and gays within the commodity context of media culture, it is surprising that Butler doesn't more fully explore what ramifications this might have for the 'hyperbolic mimicry' of gender. We could consider, for example, the value of drag to media industries perpetually on the lookout for spectacle; or the rise of reality television texts reliant on either the narrative twist of gender deception (*There's Something About Miriam*); or makeover encounters made all the more thrilling by a close encounter with gay men (*Queer Eye for the Straight Guy*). In each case, the ramifications of the relationships between subversion and market value seem critical to any consideration of how gender misperformance might disturb the system of gender. As Sedgwick argues, the production of 'contradiction' is not immanently corrosive to heterosexual hegemony, and the capacity to disturb cannot be thought outside a consideration of who or what has the capacity to 'profit from' homo/hetero indistinction.

Queer Eye for the Straight Guy is a particularly useful text to examine in this context, both because of the breakdown of homo/hetero that it performs, as well as the apparent nod to non-normativity contained in its title. A makeover show in which five gay men makeover a different straight man each week, *Queer Eye* flirts with the boundaries of homo/hetero distinction by disrupting relations of looking between men, and by making the cultural practices imagined to belong to gay men (fashion sense, good grooming, etc.) available to straight men, via the discourse of metrosexuality. Yet, in the familiarity of its camp performance and stereotypes, its insistence that the close proximity of gay men will not threaten the straight man's masculinity, and a narrative structure that puts gay men literally in the service of maintaining the romance of heterosexuality, the text safely and assuredly maintains the boundary between gay and straight. As Melinda Kanner writes, *Queer Eye* puts 'the once provocative word "queer"' (2004: 35) at a commodified critical distance from the politicised terms in which it is imagined in queer activism. At the same time, the association with the 'provocation' that Kanner assigns to history is clearly part of its commercial appeal. As Donald Hall argues, a 'catchy and provocative term such as "queer" – especially embracing as it does all sorts of sexy transgressions and possible innovations – was practically tailor-made for the marketplace' (2003: 78).

Queer Eye seems then to enact precisely the link between 'deadening cliché' and 'subversive value to the marketplace', which Butler argues might lessen the subversive impact of a failed repetition of gender normativities. To that end, the text raises the enduring problematic of context, and/or disruptive intent, that Hennessy (however problematically) suggests Butler fails to address. Yet, the conclusion that the *Queer Eye* text is not queer threatens to impose a universalised and definitive understanding as to what queer can refer to, an imposition seemingly at odds with the indeterminacy that is so central to the term. In her discussion of the commodification of subversion, Butler refuses once again to articulate any criterion of authenticity for what might be considered genuinely subversive. She suggests, instead, that such enterprises 'will always fail, and ought to' (1999: xxi–xxii), and draws us back to performativity as a way of examining how 'reality' or 'authenticity' come to have that status.

In *Bodies That Matter*, in her consideration of the extent to which the contours of queerness 'can never be fully anticipated in advance' (1993: 228), Butler draws attention to the implications of the term's performative history for its political redeployment in queer theory:

> The expectation of self-determination that self-naming arouses is paradoxically contested by the historicity of the name itself: by the history of the usages that one never controlled, but that constrain the very usage that now emblematises autonomy; by the future efforts to deploy the term against the grain of the current ones, and that will exceed the control of those who seek to set the course of the terms in the present. (1993: 228)

In this reminder that the term 'queer' itself is reconstituted from its history as a (performatively) shaming insult, Butler articulates the importance of acknowledging that the meaning of queer is always contingent upon the force that makes it so. Reclaiming queer, and orientating it into resistive directions, is to perform constitutive power in order to demonstrate that the power *to* constitute oneself is a pervasive cultural fiction. Determinations that direct particular queer performances toward tests of authenticity thus risk performing an uncritical repetition of the 'conceit of autonomy' (p. 228) that Butler argues marks the politics of naming. Theorisations of queerness must begin from the recognition that the term 'queer' is itself a site of permanent contingency.

In considering the indeterminacy of queer, Butler suggests that the term 'queer' might be made to yield in the face of unanticipated tensions and critiques. At the same time, Butler identifies what one could term (queerly rendered) caveats to utilisations of queerness that redeploy it against the full context of the radicality it was initially imagined to engender. Thus, she suggests that such accommodations must take place 'without domesticating' (1993: 228) the queer project's disruptive intent. There is a delicate and crucial tension, therefore, in the articulations and acknowledgements of queer's indeterminacy. Assessments of what can count as authentically queer are enquiries seemingly asked from elsewhere than queer theory. Yet acknowledging queer's contingency must also be to risk its deployment in significations seemingly antithetical to the term's theoretical and activist origins. Considerations of this tension between mutability and uncritical co-option manifest themselves, in particular, in concerns at the commodification of queerness, and an absence of any sustained consideration of commodity culture seems a clear theoretical gap. Yet such a gap is simultaneously unsurprising, given that Butler's acknowledgement that queer theory's subversive strategies risk becoming 'deadening clichés ... through their repetition in commodity culture' (1999: xxi) is accompanied by a refusal to apply a set of criteria to authenticate some performances of subversion and to reject others. Halperin's claim that there is nothing in particular to which queer necessarily refers demonstrates that the very essence of queer is its refusal to accept that there is an essence of queer.

QUEER THEORY AND FEMINIST THEORY

In *Bodies That Matter*, Butler suggests that the 'democratising contestations' (1993: 228–9) around the meaning and usage of queer might force considerations of how the specificities of race or gender complicate its use. As a number of theorists and activists note, the everyday use of queer as an umbrella term for an array of sexual difference can effect the same universalising tendencies of the identity politics that queer theory seeks to critique. Isling Mack-Nataf, for example, comments that she is 'more inclined to use the words "black lesbian" because when I hear the word queer I think of white, gay men' (Sullivan 2003: 48). Carolyn Williams argues that, despite its ostensible status as a 'postmodern discourse of difference', queer can 'seemingly reproduce the modernist problematic of gender indifference such that the queer white male can readily take centre stage of contemporary politics of sexuality' (1997: 294) and function as a representative subject. Elizabeth Grosz draws attention to the inescapability of the importance of gender difference by maintaining that those differences do enact power differently in the expression of sexual desire, and that queer theory elides the ways in which power operates differently in relation to differently marked bodies. She argues that queer can inaccurately equate all forms of sexual oppression, without acknowledging the (arguable) complicity of some in the oppression of others:

> 'Queer' is capable of accommodating ... many of the most blatant and extreme forms of heterosexual and patriarchal power games. Heterosexual sadists, peder-asts, fetishists, pornographers, pimps, voyeurs, suffer from social sanctions: in a certain sense they too can be regarded as oppressed. But to claim an oppression of the order of lesbian and gay, women's or racial oppression is to ignore the very real complicity and phallic rewards of what might be called 'deviant sexualities' within patriarchal and heterocentric power relations. (1995: 250)

For Sheila Jeffreys, queer's accommodation of radical sexual difference, in the form of transsexuality, butch-femme, sadomasochism, and paedophilia in particular, not only overshadows the specificity of the more valid concerns of anti-homophobic politics – it also actively works against them. Arguing that 'many of the revolutionary "sexual minorities" routinely included in "queer" are scarcely a cause for celebration', Jeffreys contends that the theory and politics of queer are in fact 'antithetical' to lesbian feminism (1996: 7).

In *Unpacking Queer Politics,* Jeffreys argues that the theories and prac-tices of queer enact a 'bias' towards gay men's sexual freedom that is part of the queer enshrining of a 'cult of masculinity' (2003: 35). This cult posits the signifiers of masculinity as more covetable for lesbians than an identifi-cation with the 'woman-loving-woman' model of what Jeffreys terms the 'heyday' of lesbian feminism (pp. 1–2). Such identifications are evidenced in practices such as packing, drag kings, and female to male transsexualism, which Jeffreys defines as 'mutilating surgery and hormone consumption' (p. 1). Within her critique, such practices signal the triumph of masculine worship over 'the lesbian feminist project of ending gender hierarchy' (p. 1). For Jeffreys, masculinity is male dominance, and she argues that the goal of lesbian-feminist politics should therefore be to eliminate masculinity altogether (pp. 6–7). Her unconditional rejection of masculinity in any form (and it is not clear what she would do with femininity) necessitates that Jeffreys rejects outright any possibility that practices such as packing, butch-femme, sadomasochism or transsexuality function as legitimate erotic exchanges between women, or that the setting of such limits might be problematic.

Yet Jeffreys's uncritical invocation of the heyday of lesbian feminism masks the vocal opposition within lesbian feminism of the normativising operation of lesbian identity, and the policing of lesbian desire. As we noted at the beginning of this chapter these feminist debates are critical to the emergence of queer. As Gayle Rubin puts it:

> By the 1970s, almost every sexual variation was described somewhere in feminist literature in negative terms with a feminist rationalization. Transsexuality, male homosexuality, promiscuity, public sex, transvestism, fetishism, and sadomasochism were all vilified within a feminist rhetoric, and some causal primacy in the creation and maintenance of female subordination was attributed to each of them. (Rubin and Butler 1997: 83)

Thus in 'Thinking Sex', Rubin seeks to demonstrate that the system that sustains 'female subordination' is also the system that sustains norms around sexual practice, and that therefore insists on the normative parameters of sexual identity. The stratification of sexuality, Rubin contends, is the basis for all sexual persecution, and feminist condemnation of SM or cross-generational sexual encounters (for example) as a result shares untenable connections with far more conservative agendas (1984: 298). 'Thinking Sex' thus seeks to move the sex-war debates away from issues of inclusion or legitimacy around lesbian identity, and towards an exploration of the ideological work that sustains the possibility *of* exclusion through the system of sexual identity, Rubin calls for a 'radical theory of sexuality' (p. 293) that would counter the oppressive effects of sexual stratification. This 'theory of sexuality' would take as its first task a thorough interrogation of the very notion of sexuality, and particularly of sexuality as a definitive marker of identity.

Given that such an interrogation is precisely what queer theory undertakes, the trajectory from Rubin to queer theory is easy to see, as is Rubin's influence on Butler. Yet Butler argues that Rubin's call has been misappropriated in queer theory to form a methodological division between sexuality (which would be the proper object of study for queer theory) and sexual difference (which would be the proper object of study for feminism). In 'Against Proper Objects' (1997d) Butler examines how the introduction to the *Lesbian and Gay Studies Reader* (Abelove et al. 1993) distinguishes between the field it seeks to represent and the field of feminism. It does so, Butler argues, by collapsing gender into sex (with the assertion that gender refers to male or female), and in the process elides the complexity of feminist theory's examination of cultural currency of such a distinction in a heteropatriarchal context. While feminist theory framed in these terms examines the effects of male/female, lesbian and gay studies (which in the context of this anthology is, effectively, queer theory) will succeed feminism and take as its proper object the discursive production of sex and sexuality (1997d: 6–7). The consequence of this, Butler argues, is that:

> the ambiguity of sex as act and identity will be split into univocal dimensions in order to make the claim that the kind of sex that one *is* and the kind of sex that one *does* belong to two separate kinds of analysis: feminist and lesbian/gay respectively. (p. 7, emphasis in original)

Such a position is clearly at odds with the relationship that Butler articulates between the materialisation of sexual difference, and the heterosexual matrix of intelligibility that this materialisation occurs within. One of the consequences of such a move is the implicit reinscription of masculinity as normative:

> If sexuality is conceived as liberated from gender, then the sexuality that is 'liberated' from feminism will be one which suspends the reference to masculine and feminine, reinforcing the refusal to mark that difference, which is the conventional way in which the masculine has achieved the status of the 'sex' which is one. Such a 'liberation' dovetails with mainstream conservatism and with male dominance in its many and various forms. (p. 23)

Thus while Butler acknowledges that the gender subversion she politicises in *Gender Trouble* will not inevitably destabilise the normative expectations of sexuality, the refusal of a 'causal or structural link' between gender and sexuality in the analyses of either threatens to simultaneously render an important 'dimension of how homophobia works' (1999: xiii–xiv) invisible to anyone working to displace it.

Such a position also erases and effaces the extent to which queer theory emerges as, and within, the politicising of sex within feminism, as the example of Rubin's essay demonstrates. In the introduction to *Feminism Meets Queer Theory* (in which 'Against Proper Objects' appears), Elizabeth Weed wonders if a more 'faithful' title might be 'feminist theorists meet the feminism of queer theory', because the version of feminism offered within queer theory is 'a strange feminism, stripped of its contentious elements, its internal contradictions, its multiplicity' (1997: ix). Routinely installed in place of this diverse field, according to Butler, is a desexualised feminism that contains only a scant critique of the heteronormative conditions within which gender oppression emerges. The example she repeatedly cites is that of the ways in which Catherine MacKinnon's work (especially her work in opposition to pornography) comes to appear as paradigmatic of feminism as such (1997d: 18–19). Butler argues that MacKinnon correlates positions of gender with sexualised positions of domination and subordination. The 'rigid determinism' under which such a position is advanced 'assimilates any account of sexuality to rigid positions of domination and subordination and assimilates those positions to the social gender of man and woman' (pp. 9–10). Feminist and lesbian-feminist opposition to this constraining narrative of sexuality is removed in the methodological distinction between queer theory and feminism.

As Butler acknowledges, 'Against Proper Objects' draws on the work of Biddy Martin (Butler 1997d: 25). In her essay 'Sexualities without Gender and Other Queer Utopias', Martin welcomes queer theory's deconstruction of identity, and its moves against the constraining narratives of some feminist theory, but also argues that there is a tendency amongst some queer theorists to 'rely on their own projections of fixity, constraint, or subjection onto a fixed ground, often onto feminism or the female body, in relation to which queer sexualities become figural, performative, playful and fun' (1994: 104). Martin pays particular attention to the discursive effect of Sedgwick's separation of the study of gender from the study of sexuality. In Axiom 2 of her introduction to *Epistemology of the Closet*, Sedgwick posits that 'The study of sexuality is not coextensive with the study of gender; correspondingly, antihomophobic inquiry is not coextensive with feminist inquiry. But we can't know in advance how they will be different' (1990: 27). The discussion that follows draws on Rubin's challenge to 'the assumption that feminism is or should be the privileged site of a theory of sexuality' (1984: 307–8), to argue for a distinct field for the study of sexuality.

In Martin's analysis, Sedgwick's response unwittingly effects precisely the kinds of appropriation of Rubin that Butler describes. Martin argues that Sedgwick's analysis of feminism's sex/gender distinction collapses sex into gender and ultimately attaches it to the significations of 'biological' difference that centre on women's capacity to reproduce (1994: 107). Sexuality, in contrast, is implicitly associated with a maleness unmarked by gender (which belongs to feminism, and therefore to women). Martin describes the move as follows:

> Yet she [Sedgwick] reacts to the irreducibility of sexuality to gender by making them more distinct, even opposed to one another. This will have the consequence of making sexuality, particularly homo/hetero sexual definition for men, seem strangely exempt from the enmeshments and constraints of gender (read: women), and, thus, even from the body. The result is that lesbians, or women in general, become interesting by making a cross-gender identification or an identification with sexuality, now implicitly (though, I think, not intentionally) associated with men, over against gender and, by extension, feminism and women. (p. 107)

What Martin is interested in, in particular, is the consequences of the implicit conception of gender in negative terms for lesbians, and especially for femme lesbians. She argues that the cleaving of gender from sexuality (and their respective gender associations), and the privileging of sexuality as the space of politics, privilege 'crossing' as the only means of reconceptualising identity. As we discussed earlier, definitions of queer tend to draw attention to, and see political possibilities within, enactments of identification and desire that confound and confuse normative expectations. Thus, in her definition of queer as a 'refusal to signify monolithically', Sedgwick offers 'lesbians who sleep with men' (1993: 8) as one example of the kind of cross-identification to which this might refer. What Martin suggests is that within this type of formulation, sexuality (associated with the masculine) becomes the only means of crossing and the only means of doing or being queer. Following Martin's critique, a question that might be raised is: 'how might we understand queer in relation to lesbians who sleep with women?'

Martin's particular concern is related to where such a schema leaves the femme. The butch lesbian played out queerly as a cross-identification with the masculine is imagined to enact the erotics of queer. Yet because the femme is associated with 'passing', and because passing is imagined as normative gender practice, the femme is seemingly left to take up the signifying space of the fixity of gender. In fact, Martin argues, because gender is conceptualised as the terrain of feminism, it is the lesbian feminist who, at least, gets the politics of gender (notwithstanding their position as negatively contrasted to queer). Thus, the privileging of cross-gender identifications 'associates the cross-gender-identified lesbian with sexuality, the lesbian-feminist with gender identification, and makes the femme lesbian completely invisible' (1994: 108).

Given Butler's insistence on the impossibility of thinking sexuality apart from gender, it is perhaps unsurprising that Martin finds a more productive critique in how Butler reconceptualises the sex/gender distinction in relation to sexual identity. Martin argues that, in contrast to Sedgwick's, Butler's work 'more explicitly connects the reconfiguration of bodily gender with the possibility of discursive significations' (p. 110). As a consequence, Butler's analysis of butch/femme calls into question the boundaries of where the body ends and construction begins, and suggests that the indeterminacy of this may be part of the 'erotic interplay' (1990: 123) that constitutes butch/femme desire. The significance of this is that it is the erotic displacement of the relationship between what we understand the body to be, and the identity that such a body is assumed to have, that may work to queer effect, rather than a reliance on the way bodily signification is read, as the privileging of gender crossing seemingly assumes. The politics of passing can thus be reimagined, not as the taking up of heterosexual privilege, but in terms more akin to the notion of queer.

Related issues arise when the relationships between transgender politics and queer theory are considered. As Jay Prosser argues, queer theory tends to operate from the persistent assumption that 'transgender is queer is subversive' (2006: 262) and, as a consequence, efface the differences between the various ways of inhabiting 'transgender'. Butler considers the tensions between queer theory and both intersex and transsexual activism, particularly around 'the question of sex assignment and the desirability of identity categories' (2004: 7). As Butler notes, 'If queer theory is understood, by definition, to oppose all identity claims, including stable sex assignment, then the tension seems strong indeed' (p. 7). Yet Butler contends that queer theory's opposition to 'those who would regulate identities or establish epistemological claims of priority for those who make claims to certain kinds of identities' (p. 7) suggests that such tensions may not be as insurmountable as they, at first, may appear.

CONCLUSION

What Butler observes is that:

> The task of all these movements [transgender, queer etc.] seems to me to be about distinguishing among the norms and conventions that permit people to breathe, to desire, to love, and to live, and those norms and conventions that restrict or eviscerate the conditions of life itself ... The critique of gender norms must be situated within the context of lives as they are lived and must be guided by the question of what maximizes the possibilities for a livable life, what minimizes the possibility of unbearable life or, indeed, social or literal death. (2004: 8)

That observation, coming as it does in *Undoing Gender,* the most recent work by Butler on gender, demonstrates how that recent work increasingly emphasises that queer is, first and foremost, a response to the violence performed by the operations and regulatory mechanisms of power. In its consideration of what is at stake for those bodies not recognisable within heteronormative regimes, Butler's later work is often characterised by the attempt to think through, analyse and identify the processes and techniques of symbolic violence. Her work on transgender, in particular, is marked by an urgency which we can connect to her assertion that:

> The harassment suffered by those who are 'read' as trans or discovered to be trans cannot be underestimated. They are part of a continuum of the gender violence that took the lives of Brandon Teena, Mathew Shephard, and Gwen Araujo. (p. 6)

Butler understands symbolic violence as something that is integral to power: the arguments, theories, examples and evidence that are brought to bear upon this area of inquiry, and the related issue of the extent to which symbolic violence can be engaged with or negotiated, constitute the subject of our next chapter.

FURTHER READING

Foucault, M. (2008) *The History of Sexuality* (trans. R. Hurley). London: Penguin.
Turner, W. (2000) *A Genealogy of Queer Theory*. Philadelphia: Temple University Press.
Weed, E. & Schor, N. (eds) (1997) *Feminism Meets Queer Theory*. Bloomington: Indiana University Press.

4 Symbolic violence

INTRODUCTION

To a marked extent *Excitable Speech* (1997a), and other more recent texts such as *Antigone's Claim* (2000), *Undoing Gender* (2004), *Giving an Account of Oneself* (2005) and *Precarious Life* (2006), are primarily concerned with analysing the processes and techniques that characterise symbolic violence. *Excitable Speech* could be characterised as an attempt to address and work through the issue of injurious or hate speech. It weaves across and between a number of exemplificative cases and sites, including pornography, abortion, Robert Mapplethorpe's photographs, gangsta rap lyrics, US military policy *re* (declarations of) homosexuality and, somewhat less obviously, US Supreme Court decisions and their accompanying commentaries.

The last example is particularly significant, for two main reasons. First, it clearly directs the subsequent narrative in the direction of issues such as sovereignty, and the consequences of institutional and discursive practices of naming. Second and relatedly, the choice of examples involving a cultural field (the law) that has a meta-discursive function with regard to the definition, identification and categorisation of violence produces an emphasis on the distinction between 'the power of a name to injure' and 'the efficacy with which that power is exercised' (1997a: 34). In other words, rather than treating injurious or hate speech as something that is relatively straightforward – in terms of 'this is what it is, this is who does it' – Butler situates it within a wider, Foucaltian-inflected understanding of power as 'the name that one attributes to a complexity which is not easily named' (p. 35).

INJURIOUS SPEECH

By transferring consideration of hate speech to the 'terrain of discursive power' (p. 34), Butler is working in accordance with Foucault's nominalistic position, which holds that power cannot be equated with or reduced to a name. However this move runs the risk of disappearing power – and by extension, injurious speech – altogether. If power has no name, or if the names we attach to power simply stand in for something that can't be named, how can it be analysed? Butler's response is to concentrate, not on subjects or names, but on the imbrication of the moments (when), sites (where), circumstances (why) and techniques (how) of the 'complex strategic situations' of power that produce and authorise names and categories. As she asks, if power:

> is not a certain strength with which we are endowed, is it perhaps a certain strength with which language is endowed? If it is neither, if power cannot be said to inhere in every subject as an 'endowed strength', then how might we account for those occasions in which power comes to appear precisely as that with which a subject is endowed or as that with which a name is endowed? (p. 35)

By way of exemplification, Butler refers to involve two related court cases. In the first instance a white teenager, who had burned a cross in front of a house occupied by an African-American family, was charged and eventually convicted under a St Paul City Council ordinance that made it a misdemeanour to communicate (through words or the deployment of symbols) a message 'one knows or has reasonable grounds to know arouses anger, alarm, or resentment in others' (p. 52). The decision was reversed by the conservative-dominated United States Supreme Court, on the basis of two rationales. First, the burning of the cross was deemed protected by the first Amendment – it was, the Court ruled, simply a '"viewpoint" within the "free marketplace of ideas"' (p. 53). Perhaps more significantly however, the majority also ruled 'it was unconstitutional to impose prohibitions on speech solely on the basis of the "content" or "subjects addressed" in that speech' (p. 53).

Butler concentrates on the second ruling, which effectively restricts not only what might be read as 'injurious speech', but also what constitutes speech itself. She works through the text of the majority opinion and demonstrates how the cross-burning is initially denied the status of an act of violence, only then to be appropriated, analogised and used against the original St Paul council ordinance. The ordinance is rendered, by the Supreme Court, as a kind of conflagration that does violence to, and is destructive of, the first Amendment – it is constituted as an 'incineration of free speech' (p. 55). The constitution is thus placed in a corresponding position to the African-American family, in that it is subject to a metaphorical cross-burning. Unlike the family, however, it is deemed to be under threat from the destructive ordinance. The categorisation of the family and home as not being under threat, on the other hand, is achieved by effectively stripping away any contextual detail – the socio-cultural history and significance of cross-burning, the racial and racist dimension of the communicative act, and the injury done to the family and the wider African-American community. The content is disappeared, and the action is abstracted and rendered as pure speech, as simply an expression of itself without regard to intention or consequence.

Butler's intervention not only seeks to reinstate the content of the action, more specifically it also reads the court's decision strategically and contextually. She follows her analysis of Justice Scalia's majority ruling and rationales with a reference to another Supreme Court text emanating from a Justice Stevens, who agrees with the majority decision but wants to specify certain conditions or cases in which apparently pure speech acts might constitute 'fighting words', and therefore be prohibited. However instead of directing the need for exemptions regarding, say, any form of racially motivated address that 'might be construed either as the incipient moment of injurious action or as the statement of an intention to injure' (p. 57), Stevens produces a narrative that transports the original act to a hypothetical fire burning in either a vacant lot (and thus having no serious consequence), or near an ammunition dump or gasoline pump (and thus potentially dangerous). The danger inherent in the second situation is projected as a force of 'substantial social disruption' (p. 58), including possible race riots that might set off attacks on business, public officials and even (as with the riots in Los Angeles following the Rodney King case) the field and officers of the law itself. The irony of this reversal is not lost on Butler:

> This sudden implication of the justices themselves might be construed as a paranoid inversion of the original cross-burning narrative. The original narrative is nowhere mentioned, but its elements have been redistributed throughout the examples; the fire which was the original 'threat' against the black family is

relocated first as an incendiary move against industry, then as a location in a vacant lot, and then reappears tacitly in the riot which now appears to follow from the trauma and threaten public officials. The fire which initially constituted the threat against the black family becomes metaphorically transfigured as the threat that blacks in trauma now wield against high officials. And though Stevens is on record as endorsing a construction of 'fighting words' that would include cross-burning as unprotected speech, the language in which he articulates this view deflects the question to that of the state's right to circumscribe conduct to protect itself against a racially motivated riot. (p. 59)

Butler goes on to argue that the 'contemporary conservative sensibility exemplified by the court' (p. 63) is played out in a variety of locations and initiatives, including expanding the category of what constitutes pornography, censoring art that is deemed obscene, and constructing 'coming out' as a form of 'fighting words' (p. 65). What is involved here is not just whether or not these issues and their practices, understood as acts of constrainment, irresponsible licence, incitement, false or demeaning categorisation, provocation and debasement, actually constitute violence. That is not the most important issue, or even one consideration amongst many. It may, from Butler's perspective, be a displaced question, one that can only be approached, meaningfully, through other forms and avenues of inquiry. So in the example of the burning cross, for instance, Butler takes her lead from Foucault and considers how the emergence of certain authorised statements, positions or doxa (say, with regard to what is recognised as violence, or who is seen as being disposed to be violent) can be made more explicable via the analysis of 'complex strategic situations'; in other words, by tracing the discursive histories and trajectories of names, designations and categories – fighting words, injurious speech, violence – within and across what Bourdieu (1998b) calls the field of power.

SYMBOLIC DOMINATION AND VIOLENCE

The main – even foundational – function of naming and categorising as a form of symbolic domination and violence is the production and maintenance of subjectivity, which Butler terms 'subjection' (1997b). Subjection involves technical and disciplinary processes (hailing, foreclosure and normalisation). These include the dissemination, deployment and reproduction of names, categories and discourses from and across various cultural fields, institutions, sites and texts (the courts, schools, bureaucracies, advertisements, films, etc.), all of which have specific effects and consequences commensurate with the notion of violence (the appearance and deployment of the human/non-human distinction, some groups being designated as fundamentally unrecognisable or unintelligible).

Butler follows Foucault in holding 'that we are formed in language', and consequently 'formative power precedes any decision we might make about it, insulting us from the start, as it were, by its prior power' (1997a: 2). In other words, to be hailed and categorised 'into existence', and thus rendered visible and explicable within the terms and evaluative regimes of the culture in which we are located, is to be 'called a name' (p. 2). Butler makes clear, however, that 'not all name calling is injurious' (p. 2). To be 'dominated by a power external to oneself is a familiar and agonizing form power takes' (1997b: 2), and this goes hand in hand with the further uncomfortable realisation that we are dependent on that which dominates us. However power also provides the subject with 'the very condition of its existence and the trajectory of its desire' (p. 2). Subjects are formed through a set of processes and discourses that 'paradoxically, initiates and sustains our agency' (p. 2).

This process of domination leads to us acquiring what Bourdieu (1990) calls a habitus, understood as a durable set of dispositions; or again, as history naturalised. The habitus both integrates subjects into, and facilitates their sense of belong and being at home in, the world. It works to:

> generate and organize practices and representations that can be objectively adapted to their outcomes without presupposing a conscious aiming at ends or an express mastery of the operations necessary in order to attain them. Objectively 'regulated' and 'regular' without being in any way the product of obedience to rules, they can be collectively orchestrated without being the product of the organizing action of a conductor. (1990: 53)

Practices are the result, then, of the conjuncture – always slightly 'out of synch' – between the formative dispositions of the habitus, and their objective conditions. At the same time the price of this sense of belonging is that the violence of subjection is endlessly repeated, again paradoxically, as an internalised misrecognition of our control, agency, responsibility, independence and freedom of choice and identification. It can also lead to what Bourdieu refers to as 'a kind of systematic self-deprecation, even self-denigration' (2001: 35): one example he cites is taken from his anthropological work in Algeria, specifically 'in the representations that Kabyle women have of their genitals as something deficient, ugly, even repulsive' (p. 35).

In the above example the Kabyle women's bodies come to 'know themselves' and perform accordingly, and so they are disgusted by 'their ugliness'. If this embodied and naturalised self-loathing seems difficult to accept or comprehend, or if the temptation arises to think of it as something characteristic of non-Western cultures, consider the extent to which, in the contemporary West, young women (and increasingly, men) are disposed to see their bodies as overweight, flawed, shameful or embarrassing. Such dispositions may be implicated in eating disorders such as anorexia, extreme dietary regimes, or constantly augmenting or seeking to transform their bodies by way of commodities or surgery.

Butler accepts this emphasis on the role of the body and bodily knowledge in helping to reconstitute the practical sense 'without which the social world would not be constituted as such' (1997a: 152). Her position, however, is that in arguing for what appears to be a relatively static notion of habitus:

> Bourdieu fails to recognise that a certain performative force results from the rehearsal of ... conventional formulae in non-conventional ways. The possibility of the resignification of that ritual is based on the prior possibility that a formula can break with its original context, assuming meanings and functions for which it was never intended. In making social institutions static, Bourdieu fails to grasp the logic of iterability that governs the possibility of social transformations. (1997a: 147)

With regard to the question of the production and regulation of gender identities, Butler puts forward a position that both acknowledges the force of the habitus, but argues that the process of subjection involves a more or less inevitable production of moments of difference:

> As the sedimented effect of a reiterative or ritual practice, sex acquires its notional effect, and yet, it is also by virtue of this reiteration that gaps and fissures are opened up as the constitutative instability in such constructions, as that which escapes or exceeds the norm, as that which cannot be wholly defined as fixed by the repetitive labor of that norm. This instability is the deconstituting

possibility in the very process of repetition, the power that undoes the very effects by which 'sex' is stabilized, the possibility to put the consolidation of the norms of 'sex' into a potentially productive crisis. (1993: 9–10)

Butler takes Bourdieu's insight that the habitus is always out of synch with regard to objective structures and discourses, and adds to it the notion of iteration as necessarily breaking with the templates of subjectivity. The fact that subjectivities have to be negotiated and renegotiated, for Butler, means that the seamless operation of the habitus is always marked, to some extent, by an awareness of its contingent nature. At the same time to be interpellated as a child, blind or visually impaired, woman, gypsy, white or Muslim is to be tied into a set of discursive trajectories that will produce category definitions we can't control and don't necessarily accept, and which will be modified or even transformed across different contexts and cultural fields and, importantly, over time. Consequently this will determine how we are viewed and treated by others, and what paths are opened and closed to us. Children growing up in migrant or refugee families, for instance, often become acutely aware of the differences in evaluative regimes with regard to cultural, ethnic or racial markers (skin colour, religion, clothing, language, accent, food, forms of behaviour, sport allegiances, familial relationships and hierarchies) across the worlds of their familial and host cultures. Moreover, they are forced into a choice (which is, in the end, no choice at all) between the violence that comes with being an outsider in the host culture (arising from difficulties or rejections encountered at school, in sporting contexts, in romantic or sexual relationships), and the violence that accompanies familial or cultural alienation (parental disapproval, a loss of community support, etc.).

PRECARIOUS LIFE

A kind of affective distance is required in order to remain inured from the pain and anxieties consequent of acts of symbolic violence. In *Precarious Life* (2006) Butler employs Emmanuel Levinas's theories as a means of helping to understand the contemporary 'domain of representation where humanization and dehumanization occur ceaselessly' (p. 140). What is at stake in cultural representations is the category and status of the human and, by extension, the non-human; and as with the example of injurious speech and the cross-burning, Butler's approach is to produce a detailed theoretical account and analysis of the techniques by which this distinction is brought about.

This is done via a discussion of Levinas's notion of the 'face' of the other, a figure which cannot speak in its own right, but which conveys the Biblical Commandment-as-imperative 'Thou shalt not kill', 'without precisely speaking it' (Butler 2006: 132). This face is not just a representation of a human face; for a start it need not be human, and the notion of the face can stand in for 'the human back, the craning of the neck, the raising of the shoulder blades ... And these bodily parts ... are said to cry and sob and scream, as if they were a face' (p. 133). The sounds of suffering emanating from, or associated with, this face are meant to generate a response and awakening to 'what is precarious in another life or, rather, the precariousness of life itself' (p. 134). The situation is somewhat complicated, however, because in Levinas's account what accompanies this precariousness of life, and the injunction not to kill, is a temptation to take advantage of the other's vulnerability and to obliterate them. The account that Butler provides by way of explanation is that the other is read as a threat to my existence, as a cause of anxiety, and because that face 'represents a menace, I must preserve myself to defend my life' (p. 136). These twin but antithetical imperatives ('not to kill', 'to destroy') are the cause of an 'ethical anxiety' (p. 136) understood as the basis of any relation with the other, and the situation of discourse itself:

> There is fear for one's own survival, and there is anxiety about hurting the Other, and these two impulses are at war with each other, like siblings fighting. But they are at war with each other in order not to be at war ... the non-violence that Levinas seems to promote does not come from a peaceful place, but rather from the constant tension between the fear of undergoing violence and the fear of inflicting violence. I could put an end to my fear by obliterating the other, although I would have to keep obliterating ... Levinas explains, though, that murdering in the name of self-preservation is not justified, that self-preservation is never a sufficient condition for the ethical justification of violence. (p. 136)

Nor, Butler suggests, is it in any sense a pragmatic or realistic course of action: as she points out, in the Biblical example cited by Levinas, the temptation for Jacob to annihilate Esau and his host of 400 would set off a necessarily ongoing cycle of violence – 'they all have family and friends, if not a nation or two behind them' (p. 137). Moreover the situation and possibility of discourse is at stake here: to obliterate the other is to put paid to language 'and the conditions of address' (p. 139), that foundational violence of being given a name and called into existence.

What looks like a highly theoretical and abstracted line of inquiry actually functions as a prelude to Butler's quite practical engagement with the US media's coverage of the invasions of Iraq and Afghanistan, which she characterises as a form of foregrounding 'against a background of effacement' (p. 141). She refers, by way of example, to the:

> faces of the Afghan girls who stripped off, or let fall, their burkas ... I visited a political theorist who proudly displayed these faces ... as a sign of democracy. A few days later I attended a conference in which I heard a talk about the important cultural meanings of the burka, the way in which it signifies belonging-ness to a community and religion, a family, an extended history of kin relations, an exercise of modesty and pride, a protection against shame, and operates as well as a veil behind which, and through which, feminine agency can and does work. The fear of the speaker was that the destruction of the burka, as if it were a sign of repression, backwardness or ... a resistance to cultural modernity itself, would result in a serious decimation of Islamic culture and the extension of US assumptions about how sexuality and agency ought to be organized and represented. (2006: 142)

Images of the invasion of Afghanistan and the 'suddenly bared faces' (p. 143) of the Afghan women are brought together within a narrative of the other 'becoming human' – a narrative augmented by and partly justified through the name of feminism, and which functions to 'cover over and derealize' other 'scenes of pain and grief' (p. 143). The scenes Butler cites clearly refer to the suffering occasioned by the hundreds of thousands of Iraqis, Afghans and invading troops killed during and after the two invasions; the terror of being forced to live in a war zone; and the lives, careers, relationships and hopes extinguished by any number of random shootings, stray bombs or 'unfortunate', 'regrettable' or 'unconfirmed' incidents. It might also extend to the camps and detention centres throughout the world where refugees suffer the final violence of being denied the category and status of the refugee, based on legal technicalities (they are citizens of countries that have now been 'liberated', etc.). In a sense all these scenes of effacement are linked to, and the pre-requisite of, images of burkas being shed (designating progress); children being given food by American soldiers in Baghdad (security and happiness); firemen amongst the ruins of the Twin

Towers (heroism); and women visiting beauty parlours in Kabul (freedom). Taken together they constitute, in Butler's words, the 'triumphalist images that give us the idea of the human with whom we are to identify' (p. 145). At the same time these images are also juxtaposed, in the media, with the represented faces of Osama bin Laden, Yasser Arafat and Saddam Hussein, who are clearly figures, not of effacement, but of 'disidentification' (p. 143), standing in as they do for terror, deception and contemporary tyranny, respectively (p. 141).

Returning to Levinas's notion of the face as the site and means of the recognition of the human, Butler asks if all the images/faces described above 'humanize in each and every instance' (p. 143). She reiterates that it is not a question of the face simply representing and establishing what is human, but rather that the human is to be recognised in the play between the attempt at establishing a template for the human, and the failure to do so. In other words, the human is what is shown as beyond representation; it is that which 'limits the success of any representational practice' (p. 144). To attempt to capture the human in any representation, then, is necessarily to lose it.

The heroic firefighters of the Twin Towers, and the American soldiers handing out food to children, are images that are meant to stand in for and capture what Butler calls 'the paradigmatically human' (p. 143). The Afghan women dropping their burkas or visiting beauty parlours, and the crowd toppling the statue of Saddam Hussein, capture the human in the sense that they show the process of becoming human – while the actual human stands behind them as an aspiration, imperative and locus of identification. With the images of bin Laden, Arafat and Saddam, on the other hand, aspirations lie elsewhere: the imperative is to obliterate, and we are required to disidentify with what is patently evil. The absent images of the pain and suffering occasioned by the war (the casualties of the wars of liberation, the refugees) have no place within authorised or official (or even mainstream media) forms of representation. In contradistinction to Levinas's notion of the face:

All of these images seem to suspend the precariousness of life; they either represent American triumph, or provide an incitement for American military triumph in the future. They are the spoils of war or the targets of war ... we might say that the face is, in every instance, defaced, and that this is one of the representational; and philosophical consequences of war itself. (2006: 143)

In *Precarious Life* Butler cites a number of contemporary or recent moments, situations and contexts (America after September 11; the war on terror; the invasions of Iraq and Afghanistan; the attempted identification, in American academic circles, of a connection between criticism of Israel and anti-Semitism) where the relation between the manifestation, and a concomitant understanding, of the precariousness of life is not just a marked absence. Instead fear, threats, destruction, death and violence combined to produce strident public and media articulations of self-righteousness and certainty, the endorsement of absolute or universal values, and intolerance towards dissent or any kind of critical thought. Butler argues that in the United States the grief that accompanied the events of September 11 gave rise, not to political reflection and a reconsideration of First World privilege (Why do they hate us? What violence or injury has been done that could provoke this response?), but rather to the revival of 'anachronistic ... and invidious' (2006: 2) distinctions and binaries (East/West, civilisation/barbarism, etc.). The war on terror provided the most obvious example of this type of practice: in a sense it started with George W. Bush's binary-producing proposition that 'Either you're with us or you're with terrorists' (p. 2), which attempted to foreclose any discussion regarding the terms (terrorism, terrorist) used to frame and categorise sides, groups and participants. Promoting or engaging in such a discussion (in other words, challenging the terms of engagement) elicited public and political denunciation and ridicule, if media censorship didn't deny entry into the highly regulated public sphere in the first place.

Butler demonstrates how the appropriation and manipulation of America's grief regarding the losses experienced on September 11, and its role as a catalyst for further violence and effacement, was manifested in any number of disparate incidents, including the move to suspend civil liberties with regard to the indefinite detention and torture of prisoners in Guantanamo Bay; and New York City mayor Rudolph Giuliani's refusal to countenance or even consider the idea of a state of moral equivalence between those killed in the Twin Towers, and the considerably greater number of Palestinians 'slaughtered at the hands of Israelis' (p. 12). This process was facilitated and even exacerbated by the American (and Western) media. Clearly it was 'doing its bit for the war', for example by showing missiles and smart bombs zeroing in on, and destroying, so-called targets in Iraq and Afghanistan (villages, bridges, military compounds), while accompanying these visuals with testimonies to the power, efficacy and righteousness of the actions, largely through the reproduction of military or state discourses about collateral damage, or missions being accomplished. In a sense this took political and military events out of the real, and lodged them within a visual fantasy space not altogether removed from the genre of (military or violent) computer games. The footage was produced in such a way that the dehumanising effect of a phrase like 'collateral damage' was transferred to visual text: television footage showed technology in action, but not the scenes of dismembered bodies or hospitalised civilians that were consequent of that technology. With CNN and Fox in particular, and the American press in general, in the reporting of the wars in Iraq and Afghanistan, American and allied acts of violence did not attract:

> graphic coverage … and so they remain acts that are justified in the name of self-defence, but by a noble cause, namely, the rooting out of terrorism. At one point during the war against Afghanistan, it was reported that the Northern Alliance may have slaughtered a village: Was this to be investigated and, if confirmed, prosecuted as a war crime? When a bleeding child or dead body on Afghan soil emerges in the press coverage, it is not relayed as part of the horror of war, but only in the service of a criticism of the military's capacity to aim its bombs right. (2006: 6)

In the face of this kind of policy and its constitutive attitudes, Butler pursues three closely related lines of inquiry: the first analyses the relationship between loss, mourning and melancholia; the second considers how and why 'certain forms of grief become nationally recognised and amplified, whereas other losses become unthinkable and ungrievable' (2006: xiv); and the third, a direct outcome of the work of the previous two, addresses the question of how contemporary instances and examples of exposure to violence and loss might serve as a basis for community.

MOURNING AND MELANCHOLIA

Butler's initial point of focus is Freud's attempts to theorise mourning and melancholia, which he both distinguishes between and correlates (Freud 1987). They are distinguished in the sense that the former is characterised as a relatively functional and non-pathological response to a loss (involving everything from the death of a loved one to the extinguishing of national liberty), while melancholia is both conventionally non-functional (it involves a withdrawal from the world, responsibilities, regard for the self or others, etc.), and possibly pathological. With mourning, time accomplishes a detachment from the object: Freud wonders that this 'painful unpleasure is taken as a matter of course by us' (p. 253), but it appears to be justified in an economic sense, in that once the process of mourning is completed 'the ego becomes free and uninhibited again' (p. 253). The same economic rationale is entirely absent from melancholia; not only is the process maintained across time without regard to social imperatives, but also it is unclear as to exactly what has been lost. Melancholia-as-psychic-process is not only devoid of any semblance of logic or utility – its very origin and context of provocation, and the question of what is at stake, remains enigmatic:

> In mourning ... the inhibition and loss of interest are fully accounted for by the work of mourning ... In melancholia, the unknown loss will result in a similar internal work and will therefore be responsible for the melancholic inhibition. The difference is that the ... melancholic inhibition displays something else which is lacking in mourning – an extraordinary diminution in ... self-regard, an impoverishment of ... ego on a grand scale. In mourning it is the world that has become poor and empty; in melancholia it is the ego itself. The patient represents his ego to us as worthless, incapable of any achievement and morally despicable; he reproaches himself, vilifies himself and expects to be cast out and punished. (1987: 254)

Freud notes that, contrary to expectation, the melancholic subject is also frequently manic, moving quickly from one discharge of emotion to another. The imbrication of these two states or pathologies seems to make melancholia more explicable, and bring it closer to the economic regime associated with mourning. This manic subject demonstrates liberation from the object of suffering 'by seeking like a ravenously hungry man for new object-cathexes' (p. 264); this is the inflection or facility by which mourning and melancholia can be brought together as related processes whereby one (lost) object is simply exchanged for another. Eventually, however, Freud begins to reverse his thinking on this matter: instead of melancholia being reappropriated into the logic of mourning, understood as a socially functional form of behaviour, the notion of mourning as a kind of necessary process that runs its course is rendered problematical in that, as with melancholia, there is no trace 'of the economic condition for a phase of triumph' (p. 264). This invalidates or at least renders problematic the explanation that mourning is characterised by a straightforward inter-changeability of objects tied to 'a kind of promiscuity of libidinal aim … as if full substitutability was something for which we might strive' (Butler 2006: 21).

If an explanation of mourning (understood as a grieving occasioned by a recognisable loss) and melancholia (a similar sense of loss, but without a concomitant objective correlative) isn't explicable in any obvious economic sense (p. 21), perhaps it needs to be sought in what Butler refers to as the 'enigmatic dimension' of unfathomable loss (p. 22). Her point is that all forms of subjection involve a dispossession or violence of some kind, and this is often not retrievable, nor something we can bring easily to consciousness, for at least three reasons. First, a great many things are necessarily closed off when we are constituted and categorised as subjects – including control of what we are and our socio-cultural trajectory, as well as various forms of reflexive knowledge that would enable us to recognise these situations as something other than willed, natural or inevitable. Second, to be produced as a subject is at the same time to be involved with and constituted out of (and therefore partly lost to) somebody or something else – a loss which is doubled and then redoubled when that someone or something else is taken away from us, and we lose the ties that help constitute us. Third and finally, the process of naming is frequently associated with, or accompanied by, a naturalised abjection; in such cases we lose our status as human beings and are denied the right to identify with others, to recognise ourselves, and to grieve. All three of these reasons are pertinent both to the issue of the relation between mourning, melancholia and loss, as well as to the question of why 'certain forms of grief become nationally recognised and amplified, whereas other losses become unthinkable and ungrievable' (p. xiv).

NORMALISATION AND FORECLOSURE

The two terms that are central to this notion of subjection as a form of domination and violence are 'normalisation' and 'foreclosure'. Butler follows Foucault in understanding subjectivity as a consequence of regulatory power and apparatuses that operate to produce socio-cultural norms. Gender is one obvious example and site of normalisation, but each and every socio-cultural category (age, ethnicity, class, profession, etc.) is characterised by, and constituted from, the deployment and dissemination of authorised regulatory norms. Norms are usually implied rather than explicitly articulated; they are neither rules nor laws, and are discernible 'most clearly and dramatically in the effects that they produce' (Butler 2004: 41). Moreover, and as Foucault makes clear, regulatory norms are not to be understood simply as forms of prohibition or constraint; rather, they are productive in the sense that they allow, facilitate and dispose socio-cultural practices, and render those practices as intelligible or otherwise. With regard to gender categories, for instance, they impose a 'grid of legibility on the social' and define:

> the parameters of what will and will not appear within the domain of the social. The question of what it is to be outside the norm poses a paradox for thinking, for if the norm renders the social field intelligible and normalizes the field for us, then being outside the norm is in some sense being defined still in relation to it. To be not quite masculine or not quite feminine is still to be understood exclusively in terms of one's relationship to the 'quite masculine' and 'quite feminine'. (2004: 42)

Gender, then, is not a substance (corresponding to a particular biological set) or an attribute (stereotypes about women being sensitive and caring, and men being logical and practical, etc.); rather it is the relationship between a discursive apparatus and a set of categories, on the one hand, and socio-cultural practices, performances, histories, habitus, dispositions, imperatives and bodily hexis that result from and are understood and recognised in terms of those categories, on the other. It constitutes a form of symbolic violence because everything outside those parameters is foreclosed; and any biological or cultural combination not commensurate with gender norms is rendered unintelligible, and consequently, not really human.

According to Lacan, subjectivity is predicated on foreclosure, a term that is not without its theoretical difficulties. Lacan claims to have taken it from Freud: his idea of foreclosure more or less corresponds to Freud's use, across different texts and case studies, of the concepts of repudiation, refusal, repression, rejection, suppression and disavowal (Laplanche and Pontalis 1988: 166–7). For both Freud and Lacan, foreclosure is specifically linked to, or comparable with, the notion of psychosis; that is to say, in one sense it is a disavowal of reality. In the case study of the 'Wolf Man', Freud (1987) describes a situation where the male patient as a child witnesses his parents copulating, and becomes aware of the fact that his mother does not have a penis. What is at issue here for the patient is the reality of his own forthcoming and necessary castration at the hands of the father, and his inability to come to terms with this 'intolerable perception':

> The disavowal which is the common response of the child, the fetishist and the psychotic to the supposed 'reality' of the absence of the penis in the woman is understood as a refusal to admit the 'perception' itself and ... to draw the inevitable conclusion from it and accept ... castration ... Freud postulates two modes of defence: rejection of an instinctual demand from the external world' and 'disavowal of a portion of the real external world' ... These two explanations ... were not mutually exclusive for Freud: the withdrawal of cathexis ... is also a withdrawal of significance. (Laplanche and Pontalis 1988: 167–8)

Lacan refers to two 'complementary operations ... introduction into the subject ... and ... expulsion from the subject' (Laplanche and Pontalis 1988: 168). Introduction equates with a symbolic acceptance of the consequences of, and an adherence to, the law of the father; and expulsion with a necessary repression or sending away of this initial primary process, which comes to constitute 'the Real insomuch as this is the domain which subsists outside symbolisation' (p. 168). This process allows access to the symbolic order and the status of a normal subject. Foreclosure, on the other hand, consists 'in not symbolizing what ought to be symbolized ... it is a "symbolic abolition"' (p. 168). In effectively maintaining 'his relation to the mother through an identification with her', the subject fails to represent and accept the law of the father, and thus cannot 'be positioned within the symbolic with a stable, ongoing position' (Grosz 1990: 164). The subject is dispossessed of socio-psychic stability through the recurrence of hallucinations, emanating from the Real, of desires that have been sent away; and undone by attachments and forms of love that are outside gender-as-norm, and therefore impossible. This subject is:

> fundamentally threatened by the spectre of this ... love's reappearance and remains condemned to reenact that love unconsciously, that impossibility, orchestrating that threat to one's sense of 'I'. 'I' could not be who I am if I were to love in the way that I apparently did, which I must, to persist as myself, continue to deny and yet unconsciously reenact in contemporary life with the most terrible suffering as its consequence. The traumatic repetition of what has been foreclosed from contemporary life threatens the 'I'. (Butler 1997b: 8–9)

Antigone's Claim (2000) constitutes Butler's most comprehensive and worked-through attempt to address this relation between foreclosure, and symbolic domination and violence. Antigone is a figure from fiction, most notably Sophocles's fifth century BC drama about the clash between the eponymous heroine and daughter of Oedipus, and Creon, her uncle and the King of Thebes. Creon has issued an edict that condemns to death anyone who provides his nephew Polyneices with a proper funeral and burial, while Antigone insists on burying her brother, despite the cost.

Antigone's 'choice' has generally been read by cultural commentators as an example of civil disobedience and a defiance of the power of sovereignty, but also by feminists as enacting a refusal of patriarchy; by Hegel as a representative of kinship and blood ties and politics made anachronistic by the emergence of the state; and by Lacan as a necessary negativity, a kind of enabling stage transitional to, and which helps inaugurate, the order of the symbolic, law and norms. For Butler, however, Antigone's story (and her death) can be read as an example of foreclosure-as-violence, a determination of 'what forms of kinship will be intelligible, what kind of lives can be countenanced as living' (2000: 29).

If Creon's Thebes is an incipient version of the society of the regulatory norm, then Antigone is out of time and place. She is first and foremost, and in everything she does, scandalous – as the daughter of Oedipus, she already has a history that presages her fate: she confronts and contests sovereign authority, she acts and performs like, and takes the positions and roles of, a man in society; she privileges primitive blood ties over the more modern political regime of the state; her sense of community and duty is focused on kin rather than the wider polis; and finally and most importantly, her motives and desires can be read as more than sisterly affection, verging on a violation of what the anthropologist Claude Lévi-Strauss characterises as the universal prohibition against incest that supposedly links nature and culture (Butler 2000).

Butler notes with interest that this incestuous dimension to the play/story is not addressed or even acknowledged by many influential commentators and theorists: Lacan, for instance, predictably empties the relationship of any content (Antigone's desire is largely characterised in terms of a formal defiance of regulatory norms); while for Hegel it is marked by a complete absence of any desire (Butler 2000). Butler queries the claims, derived from Lévi-Strauss's work, of the universality, efficacy and socio-cultural function of the incest prohibition. She is particularly concerned with the Lacanian-influenced psychoanalytical position that understands that prohibition as instituting a regime of marked and unmarked positions within the symbolic order, separate from the level of any specific social content. So just as, for Lacanian theory, the phallus is not a penis, so too kinship positions are not identifiable with, or reducible to, gender relations, sexual practices or bodily configurations. From this perspective the incest prohibition is something primordial that makes the social possible, and it clearly organises, orients and evaluates, in one way or another, the field of social desire. However, those social practices and desires that it produces are only really explicable in structural, rather than social, cultural and/or political, terms; in other words, the idea is that there is nothing outside the structure.

The rule or law of the incest prohibition provides a structuralist explication of social practices and relationships that is exhaustive and continuous. That is why Lacanian psychoanalysis can claim that incest is, in fact, impossible – because there is nothing to happen. Incestuous desire is a desire brought into being through the structural relations of the symbolic order, which effectively arranges our places within the social; in other words, the desire associated with incest is the product of a mechanism. Foucault demonstrates, more generally with regard to disciplinary and normative regimes, that the rule which categorises also creates both the norm and its other. As Butler asks, apropos of the incest prohibition, could such a rule:

> operate, however effectively, without producing and maintaining the spectre of its transgression? Do such rules produce conformity, or do they also produce a set of social configurations that exceed and defy the rules by which they are occasioned? I take this question to be what Foucault has underlined as the pro- ductive and excessive dimension of the rule of structuralism. To accept the final efficacy of the rule in one's theoretical descriptions is thus to live under its regime, accept the force of its edict, as it were. (2000: 17)

For Butler, an inability or refusal to think against or outside a normative rule effectively reinscribes that rule, and to some extent *Antigone's Claim* is Butler's attempt to articulate how psychoanalytical universalising of the Oedipus complex and the prohibition against incest (and symptomatically, Lacan's readings of *Antigone*) redoubles the normative violence that has Antigone 'already living in the tomb prior to any banishment there' (p. 77). Antigone's unwillingness to perform as a normal woman, her refusal to become a wife and a mother, the many manifestations of her 'wavering gender'

(p. 76), and her eventual suicide, all render her unintelligible to the society of which she is ostensibly a part. To return to the concepts of mourning and melancholia: Antigone is 'trying to grieve, to grieve openly ... under conditions in which grief is explicitly prohibited by an edict' (p. 79), but she is confronted by 'a socially instituted foreclosure of the intelligible in which unintelligible life emerges in language as a living body might be interred into a tomb' (pp. 80–1).

The law, notions of community, and the discursive and normative status and function of the concept of the human are already and always predicated on violence and exclusion. We can refer to and make claims upon them, but such linguistic practices are invariably characterised by a catachresis (the strained use of a word) and chiasmus (a crossing over or reversal of elements) that demonstrate the dubious, unsustainable or transitional status of concepts designated as natural and universal – even as they proliferate and take on the status of socio-political doxa. Butler refers to Giorgio Agamben's observation that, increasingly in the contemporary world:

> populations without full citizenship exist within states ... their ontological status as legal subjects ... suspended. These are not lives that are being genocidally destroyed, but neither are they being entered into the life of the legitimate community in which standards of recognition permit for an attainment of humanness. How are we to understand this 'shadowy realm', which haunts the public sphere, which is precluded from the public constitution of the human ... Is this not a melancholy of the public sphere? (2000: 81)

The reference here, or at least one obvious reference, is to Palestinians living within territories controlled by the state of Israel. In *Precarious Life* (2006) Butler devotes a chapter to a consideration of how Israeli state violence is represented, and rendered explicable, via a series of positions and discourses that militate against recognition of, and effectively work to deny, the 'ontological status' of Palestinians. Her point of departure is a discursive exchange centred around a speech made in 2002 by Lawrence Summers, the President of Harvard, in which he decried the increase in 'Profoundly anti-Israeli views' emanating from 'progressive intellectual communities', and stated that such actions were 'anti-Semitic in their effect, if not their intent' (Butler 2006: 101). Summers denied that his intention was to censor or inhibit public discussion of what was clearly an important and divisive political issue in the United States and elsewhere; but as Butler suggests, his words 'nevertheless exercised a chilling effect on political discourse, stoking the fear that to criticize Israel during this time is to expose oneself to the charge of anti-Semitism' (p. 102).

CATEGORISING VIOLENCE

To some extent this chapter in *Precarious Life* is about political censorship both in a general sense, and more specifically (and in terms of Summers's intervention, locally) with regard to initiatives such as the petition drafted by MIT and Harvard academics opposed to Israel's treatment of Palestinians. However it also deals with what we might term the technical and structural processes whereby forms of overt violence (bombings of various kinds, the wholesale slaughter of families, the denial or suspension of political rights) come to be categorised as such (and denounced); or alternatively are treated as understandable, aberrations or of an entirely different order to what is normally categorised as violence – and therefore less likely to demand attention, comment, explanation or justification.

Much of the work of *Precarious Life* and *Frames of War* (2009) is taken up with identifying and analysing these structural and structuring processes that bring about certain reality effects. More specifically they make something into violence, or alternatively, cause it (as a reflex) to disappear, to go unrecognised, to be passed over. As Butler writes:

> I am seeking to draw attention to the epistemological problem raised by this issue of framing: the frames through which we apprehend or, indeed, fail to apprehend the lives of others as lost or injured ... are politically saturated. They are themselves operations of power. They do not unilaterally decide the conditions of appearance but their aim is nevertheless to delimit the sphere of appearance itself. (2009: 1)

If the categorisation (and therefore, designation) of violence can be understood as having a structural dimension, and to be at least partly a function of framing, then the key to this organisation of the similar as the different is the discursive inflection and deployment of what Claude Lefort (1986) calls capitalised ideas, in this case 'anti-Semitism' and 'victim'. Two technical points are worth noting: first, capitalised ideas organise other discourses, terms and categories. Such ideas or terms have acquired a discursive value that overcomes, or takes precedence over, other terms. This allows them to authorise patterns and relations of resemblance or dissimilarity, and to establish hierarchies based on points of resemblance or commensurability. By way of example, any interpretive or evaluative discussion (and this is true across cultural fields as disparate as law, philosophy, politics, religion and economics) of practices associated with or productive of pain or suffering inevitably starts with, and is then usually directed by, the logics, imperatives, narratives and meanings (currently) associated with the capitalised idea of 'the human'. So any attempt to draw a comparison between the slaughter of people in a concentration camp and sheep in an abattoir, for instance, would be unthinkable as long as the organising concept or principle was the term 'human' rather than 'life form'. Second, capitalised ideas are empty ideas; that is to say their content is naturalised without being natural in any way; is usually the subject of intense and ongoing disputation, agonistics or debate; and is transformed or modified by the field of power.

In her detailed analysis of the way the terms 'victim' and 'anti-Semitism' are deployed by Summers and by other participants (politicians, peace groups, and most importantly the media) in the accompanying debate, Butler demonstrates just how closely the terms are discursively interwoven, and how this interweaving allows Summers to claim Israeli policy 'should be vigorously challenged' (2006: 102), while simultaneously denying the possibility of such a course of action. The logic is straightforward enough: Israel is cast as the eternal victim, and the discourse on Israel has to be commensurate with the doxa emanating from the Israeli government, only falling into two categories of practice – one either provides support for, or engages in racist (anti-Semitic) attacks on, the victim.

This restriction on the use of the term 'victim' ensures that there is no authorised facility within the US public sphere (or indeed throughout the West) that would allow it to be associated with those Palestinians who are subject to Israeli violence. Even in the case of the most obvious and egregious examples – children targeted by Israeli bombs and gunfire, civilians indiscriminately slaughtered in operations supposedly targeting militants described as terrorists, people dispossessed and rendered homeless by new settlements that are patently illegal under international law – these victims have to go under another name, or are given no name at all. Civilians killed by the Israeli military, for instance, are often displaced from inclusion in the category of victim by media reports that call into question the veracity of their status – which usually 'cannot be confirmed', or is denied by the same Israeli military, which promises to investigate such claims – effectively disappearing them. Alternatively, media reports accept, or only report, Israeli versions of events that describe the bodies as being those of militants or terrorists. Finally, Israeli acts of violence are often contextualised as being responses to Palestinian aggression, or simply self-defence; here the Palestinian casualties are precluded from victim status in advance by their presumed complicity in attacks on the state and population of Israel.

This largely unquestioned adherence, in the West, to this narrative of Israel-as-victim constitutes a form of symbolic violence in itself. As Butler points out an ethical regime cannot be based on

> the assumption that Jews monopolize the position of victim. The 'victim' is a quickly transposable term, and it can shift from minute to minute from the Jew atrociously killed by suicide bombers on a bus … historically we are now in the position in which Jews cannot be understood always and only as presumptive victims. (2006: 103)

However this is not the case, at the level of media reporting and representations, largely because the charge of 'anti-Semitism' has come to function as a discursive and structural bar within the Western public sphere and in this specific case and has been applied to any attempt 'to allow knowledge to acquire an adequate idea of itself' (Foucault 2007: 67). Butler shows how this even operates with regard to Jews who are critical of Israel, but normally would be immune from the charge of anti-Semitism:

> If we think … that to criticize Israeli violence, or to call for specific tactics that will put economic pressure on the Israeli state to change its policies, is to engage in 'effective anti-Semitism', we will fail to voice our opposition out of fear of being named as part of an anti-Semitic enterprise. No label could be worse for a Jew. The very idea of it puts fear in the heart of any Jew who knows that, ethically and politically, the position with which it would be utterly unbearable to identify is that of anti-Semite. It recalls images of Jewish collaborators with the Nazis. (2006: 103)

What Butler is referring to here is both a structure and culture of foreclosure. It is a structure in the same sense that within the Western (and particularly the American) media-dominated public sphere, any and every attempt to circulate a discourse that is critical of Israel runs up against the linguistic and ideological bar that equates Israelis with the status of victim. To hold and be defined by the status of victim is, in structural terms, to be deemed incapable of violence. If Israel is always the victim, any dispute (involving the Israeli military's violence against Palestinian civilians, American academics protesting against the dispossession or dislocation of up to three quarters of a million Palestinians, or even Jews questioning Zionism) consequently and automatically designates the other party as (in effect) a victimiser. Since Israel is equated with the role of victim largely because of the history (recent and otherwise) of anti-Semitic sentiment and violence in the West, it follows (or rather, it is prescribed) that the criticism-as-victimisation of Israel is also a form of anti-Semitism. This structural relation and its accompanying narratives give rise to a culture of paralysis and terror, which in turn works to reproduce, at a discursive and practical level, the original prescription against any criticism of Israel.

CONCLUSION

What Butler and other academics ran into when they sought to widen the debate about Israeli policies was the problem of a media-dominated public sphere that is subjected, almost exclusively, to the imperative of 'time and effect' (Bourdieu 1998a). This imperative effectively privileges the sensational, the hyperbolic and the simplistic over nuance and complexity, and substitutes and repeats an easily recognisable and unproblematic set of positions and narratives for each and every issue (the problem of nuclear weapons is exhausted by references to North Korea and Iran, terrorism is exclusively practised by 'rogue states' and Islamic fundamentalists). Allied to this is the 'invisible censorship' played out in the media, where usually only those who are willing to stick to the script (with regard to the war on terror, the global economic crisis, or Israeli policies towards Palestine) are allowed to appear and speak. To be used as an expert on television, for instance, often involves 'churning out regularly and as often as possible works whose principal function ... is to get them on television' (Bourdieu 1998a: 14). What this effectively produces is a constant stream of disinformation that enacts 'a particularly pernicious form of symbolic violence' (p. 17), because it controls 'what can and cannot be permissibly spoken out loud in the public sphere'

(Butler 2006: 127). The exclusion of critical discourses on Israel's policy towards Palestinians, as well as on other significant contemporary issues, establishes 'the boundaries of the public itself, and the public will come to understand itself as one that does not speak out, critically, in the face of obvious and illegitimate violence' (p. 127).

The question that Butler poses, in books such as *Giving an Account of Oneself* (2005), *Precarious Life* (2006) and most recently *Frames of War*, is how do we 'acknowledge or, indeed ... guard against injury and violence' (2009: 3). In our final chapter we shall consider how Butler approaches this problem, this 'ethical problem' (p. 3), of identifying and critiquing violence in its many forms, in the contemporary media-dominated public sphere.

FURTHER READING

Bourdieu, P. (2001) *Masculine Domination.* Cambridge: Polity Press.
Freud, S. (1984) *On Metapsychology.* Harmondsworth: Penguin.
Laplanche, J. & Pontalis, J. (1988) *The Language of Psychoanalysis.* London: Karnac Books.

5 Ethics

INTRODUCTION

In *Giving an Account of Oneself*, Butler engages with the work of Adorno, Foucault, Laplanche and Levinas, amongst others, in order to consider 'how it might be possible to pose the question of moral philosophy' (2005: 1). What she means by this expression, and what might be at stake in such an inquiry, is to be sought in the conjunction of the ideas, examples, arguments, positions and theories she includes in the discussion, on the one hand; and the socio-cultural climate and politics of the post-September 11 world, and the political issues (the Israeli-Palestinian conflict, media and academic censorship, the Gulf War) at the centre of *Precarious Life* (2006) and *Frames of War* (2009), on the other. In this context, giving an account of oneself involves both an ethics and a pragmatics.

Consider the situation we described in our previous chapter, where Butler and other academics sought to intervene in the public sphere debate regarding Israeli policies and practices with regard to the Palestinians. Butler relates the story of a 'Campus Watch' blacklist that identified scholars 'understood to be anti-Semitic or to be fomenting anti-Semitism' (2006: 121). Butler, amongst others, complained about not being on the list; this eventually gave rise to a story, written by Tamar Lewin from the *New York Times*, about 'the rising anti-Semitism on campus' (2006: 121). Butler describes her attempts to negotiate and keep open the meaning of their action, and the significance of what was at stake. This involved explaining to Lewin that as a progressive Jew she rejected the idea that support for Palestinian self-determination could be equated with or read as anti-Semitic; informing her that this position was held by a number of Jewish organisations; pointing out how the charge of anti-Semitism was being used to silence debate and criticism; and making it clear that those who opposed the blacklist shared a revulsion of anti-Semitism. Lewin went ahead and wrote her story without taking any of this into account. The point of the story is that within such a culture, speaking out potentially means, at best, losing the right to negotiate, refute, argue or complain about how one's speech has been interpreted or used.

Butler's work on the relationship between ethics and giving an account of oneself is strongly influenced by Foucault's later works, particularly the collected lectures and interviews from the 1980s, which explore the question of what constitutes and facilitates ethical behaviour, understood as a necessary and consistent correlation between a subject's values, accounts and practices. For Foucault this takes in and involves the notion of care of the self; the distinction between knowledge, and giving an account, of oneself; the conditions, consequences and responsibilities associated with public speech; the relation between discourse and subjectivity; the definition and function of critique; and perhaps most importantly, the Greek concept of parrhesia (which Foucault translates as 'free speech'). Giving an account of oneself, for Butler, is here largely contextualised within the wider Foucaltian engagement with 'what we could call the "critical" tradition in the West' (Foucault 2001: 170).

ETHICS AND UNIVERSALITY

A beginning is made via Theodore Adorno's critique of Max Scheler's lament for 'the destruction of a common and collective ethical ethos' (Butler 2005: 1) in contemporary Western society. For Adorno, the idea of a collective ethos is to be understood as a form of universality (or World Spirit, in Hegelian terms) that must eventually lose its efficacy and socio-ethical function. Adorno suggests that 'Once the state of human consciousness and the state of social forces of production have abandoned these collective ideas', then we can say that the 'World Spirit has ceased to inhabit them' (2005: 4). The collective ethos lives on, however, as an anachronism and simulation that imposes itself on the community. It is no longer universal in any sense, but it 'instrumentalizes violence to maintain the appearance of its collectivity' (p. 4).

One of the ways in which this now false universal maintains itself, despite being out of time, is through its discursive manifestation as ultimately repressive forms of morality and norms. One example is the capitalised idea

(Lefort 1986) of the traditional family in the West, which as a content (a married heterosexual couple with children derived from that marriage) corresponds to only a small percentage of the population, yet stands in for what a family really is and should be, and who can claim that name. Another example of this process is the elevation of particular interests to the status of the universal, as when one ethnic culture effectively 'stands in' for the nation; or when American presidents as unalike as George W. Bush and Barack Obama visit Iraq, Afghanistan or anywhere in Africa and effectively claim that they need to become free, which effectively means aspiring to become like capitalist, democratic America. In these circumstances the universal appears, in Adorno's words, 'as something violent and extraneous and has no substantial reality for human beings' (Butler 2005: 5).

The identification of the gap that is opened up between claims of universality and particular interests (that are framed as universal) constitutes the conditions for the emergence of what Adorno calls morality and moral questioning (p. 6). This questioning, however, is dependent on and enacted by subjects who are themselves necessarily within, and products of, the world of norms and discursive regimes. When the subject comes to articulate a relation to morality or moral questioning, in Butler's words comes to 'give an account of itself ... it can start with itself, it will find that this self ... must include the conditions of its own emergence' (pp. 7–8).

REFLEXIVITY, CONSCIENCE AND MORALITY

Butler considers two main explanations of the process whereby the subject can become reflective, the first derived from Nietzsche, the second from Foucault. In *On the Genealogy of Morals* (1956) Nietzsche posits reflective consciousness as arising out of an interpellation of the subject as the possible cause of violence, injury or pain with regard to another. This requires that we provide an account of the charges made against us; and we deliver up this account, under threat to some extent, in the form of a narrative that stands in for, and testifies to, our moral worth. This narrative constitutes a performance of compliance and/as cultural literacy. It is a performance of compliance because simply to respond effectively acknowledges and legitimates both the process of interpellation, and the power of the legal, social, religious or governmental regime to demand an account from its subjects. It is a performance of cultural literacy because an account or narrative will not stand unless it recognises its own place (as subservient, humble, debased, obliged and guilty to some extent), utilises the appropriate discourse (referencing responsibility, attachment and allegiance), and articulates an appropriate affective response and form of address (being transformed, living in faith, accepting the verdict, coming to a recognition, etc.).

This articulation and performance inscribes a memory upon the subject understood as a form of consciousness – which for Nietzsche equates with bad conscience. It is a bad conscience because those characteristics that are found in what Nietzsche considers the highest form of life – instincts, boldness, strength, vitality – are not just erased or subjugated, but in fact become the basis of the subject's guilt. Moreover weakness, understood as the opposite of the aforementioned vital forces and traits, is now transmuted:

> Impotence, which cannot retaliate, into kindness; pusillanimity into humility; submission before those one hates into obedience to One of whom they say that he has commanded this submission – they call him god. The inoffensiveness of the weak, his cowardice, his ineluctable standing and waiting at doors, are being given honorific titles such as patience; to be unable to revenge oneself is called to be unwilling to avenge oneself – even forgiveness ... Also there's some talk of loving one's enemy – accompanied by much sweat. (Nietzsche 1956: 180–1)

The violence, brutality and cruelty that characterised life-as-will aren't entirely disappeared. Rather, they are transformed into morality, civility, conscience and duty, and duly released precisely in those times and places when one is required to do one's duty, act righteously in accordance with one's conscience, uphold civility, and further the imposition of morality – experienced as a form of enjoyment:

> To behold suffering gives pleasure, but to cause another to suffer affords an even greater pleasure. This severe statement expresses an old, powerful, human, all too human sentiment ... There is no feast without cruelty, as man's entire history attests. Punishment, too, has its festive features. (1956: 198)

As Butler notes, Nietzsche's account of the advent of morality is both punitive-based, and predicated on a reversal of violence: since 'aggression is co-existent with life' (2005: 13), morality (in its institutionally driven manifestations) restricts life while allowing it to be played out in various non-barbaric or civilised forms (normalising the imperative to confess, naturalising guilt, institutionalising a culture of subservience). Morality gives rise to reflection, but it is as a form of reflexivity 'on the model of self-beratement' (p. 14).

The Nietzschean encounter with the other is articulated as a narrative of revenge. It is the threat of punishment from the other which gives birth to the notion of the human, which turns the natural aggression-as-vitality of life into a form of bad conscience. In other words, I take revenge both on myself (as an object of guilt and aggression) and on life itself: my morality is opposed to and restricts vitality. It manifests itself as religiosity, self-effacement, forgiveness, and the privileging of the weak, or as the severe enjoyment of the law. For Nietzsche aggression is primary to life; but the reflective turn to the human simply redirects this aggression into institutionalised and non-vitalistic forms. According to Butler, however, Nietzsche 'fails to understand the other interlocutory conditions in which one is asked to give an account of oneself' (2005: 14) – conditions and situations where otherness does not automatically or necessarily produce a response of fear and guilt.

RECOGNITION AND OTHERNESS

Butler refers to and deploys Adriana Cavarero's Levinasian account of recognition as an alternative not just to Nietzsche's 'punitive scene of Inauguration' (2005: 15); it is also set against Hegel's dyadic encounter, and Foucault's emphasis on the reflexive process of forming the self, both of which are here replaced by or subordinated to the primacy of otherness. The significant question for Cavarero and Levinas is not 'how can I gain recognition from an other' (Hegel), or 'what can I become' (Foucault), but:

'Who are you?' This question assumes that there is an other before us whom we do not know and cannot fully apprehend, one whose uniqueness and nonsubstitutability set a limit on the model of reciprocal recognition offered within the Hegelian scheme and to the possibility of knowing another more generally. (2005: 31)

The encounter with the other here functions as a form of connectivity without necessarily involving identification or empathy, and this provides the basis of subjectivity and all social activity and relations. With Nietzsche the exchange with the other results in a kind of fall, a loss of self-autonomy and the instinctive that is akin to slavery. For Cavarero what is at stake is not enslavement but a limited form of beholding: the other makes me possible, I become me because of you. The 'you' is the significant term here, opposed to and always rendered irrelevant or peripheral by a linguistic code 'based on the intrinsic morality of pronouns' (Cavarero 2000: 91). It is not the 'I' of contemporary individualism, nor is it the 'we' of revolutionary movements or even imagined communities; rather, it is a term that situates the processes of subjectivity within terms of dependence that never threaten or extinguish difference. Each 'you' is embedded in a series of intrinsically social relationships that is simultaneously a chain of singularities. From this perspective the social is predicated on an ethics without recourse or reducible to:

> empathy, identification, or confusion. Rather this ethic desires a you that is truly an other, in her uniqueness and distinction. No matter how much you are similar and constant, says this ethic, your story is never my story. No matter how much the larger traits of our life-stories are similar, I still do not recognize myself in you and, even less, in the collective we. (2000: 92)

Butler points out, however, that Cavarero's refusal of the possibility of the 'we' is undercut by her failure to show what is specific to a social singularity; in other words, if each singularity 'has no defining content', apart from its membership of a process that is 'reiterated endlessly, it constitutes a collective condition, characterizing us all equally' (2005: 35). Moreover Cavarero's account, so thoroughly distanced from Nietzsche's narrative of agonistics, misrecognition, subordination and bad conscience, fails to account for the constitutive roles of the scenes, forces and play of power, and the ways in which socio-cultural norms facilitate, dispose and delimit the processes of recognition. While our subjectivity may be derived from the condition of being 'exposed to one another in our vulnerability and singularity' (p. 31), it follows that this exposure necessarily takes a much wider, differentiated, and pedagogical form. In Foucaltian terms, norms not only 'condition the possibility of recognition' (p. 33): the specific contexts in which they are deployed (across different cultural fields, for instance) ensure that a norm always 'operates variably' (p. 33), to some extent. It follows, then, that we are disposed to seek out, value and privilege certain types of recognition over others. The exposure of the subject is played out in terms of the trajectories of different fields (government, the law, etc.) and the texts, discourses and more generally the practices of power, all of which move in time and space across the body of the subject, and in doing so dispose and evaluate different forms and practices of recognition.

GIVING AN ACCOUNT OF ONESELF: TIME AND SPACE

Modifications to supposedly universal categories (man, woman, child) are usually slow and almost unnoticeable. However since the 1980s it is clear that significant changes have taken place in the dynamics of the relation between the subject and time/place, largely brought about by the pervasive influence of the global media with regard to everyday life and public sphere activity (Appadurai 1997). Every day we experience a flow of images and information – via computers and digital technology generally, but also television and film – that is far greater, and of a different order, to what was the case thirty years ago. Arjun Appadurai has pointed out that whereas 'once improvisation was snatched out of the glacial undertow of the habitus, habitus now has to be painstakingly reinforced in the face of life-worlds that are frequently in flux' (p. 56). This sense of disorientation, already and always accentuated by the movements of what Butler refers to as 'vectors of temporality' (2005: 35), to some extent conditions the accounts one is able to provide of and about oneself.

For Butler these accounts are always alienated, given in the form of that discourse that is 'not the same as the time of my life' (2005: 36). In deconstructionist terms, the text of my account of myself is disseminated, rather than controlled or directed. Instead of moving in a pre-arranged, intended or predictable manner, or in accordance with my will, meaning always moves outward and in a variety of trajectories. Language is marked by a variety of histories and contexts that work against any attempt to stabilise meaning. Indeed as Derrida (1976) points out, language and meaning can only function precisely because they are portable; that is to say they are not reducible to, or constrained or exhausted by, any singular context. This process of the 'dispossession in language' is further accentuated 'by the fact that I give an account of myself to someone, so that the narrative structure of my account is superseded by ... the structure of address in which it takes place' (Butler 2005: 39). Moreover 'telling about myself' (p. 39) is always a practice embedded in, driven by and spoken through what we could call, following Foucault, the imperatives of normativity.

Every cultural field is not only characterised by its own discourses, but also by distinctive genres and forms of address. The rigidity of communication practices and available narratives in the military field, for instance, could be contrasted with the seemingly informal and non-directed banter and small talk of clubs and cafés; but virtually all social activities are characterised by highly conventionalised, and even ritualised, embodied codes that determine how and when one articulates an account of oneself (with regard to tone, discourse and pace), and the kinds of narratives that one can address to different subject categories (based on gender, social standing, age, etc.). Moreover, these conditions of address are themselves subject to time, and therefore not stable: the account that is facilitated, inflected or directed by one place or context will be replaced by something emanating from marginally or entirely different configurations of subject position and cultural field. For these and related reasons, what passes as a self-narrative will always be limited by, contingent upon, and derived from someone or somewhere else. As Butler writes:

> My account of myself is partial, haunted by that for which I can devise no definitive story. I cannot explain exactly why I have emerged in this way, and my efforts at narrative reconstruction are always undergoing revision. There is that in me and of me for which I can give no account. But does this mean that I am not … accountable for who I am and for what I do? If I find that … a certain opacity persists and I cannot make myself fully accountable to you, is this ethical failure? Or is it a failure that gives rise to another ethical disposition … for acknowledging a relationality that binds me more deeply to language and to you … And is the relationality that conditions and blinds this 'self' not, precisely, an indispensable resource for ethics? (2005: 40)

THE ETHICAL DISPOSITION

The ethical disposition that Butler refers to here is tied to the question of how subjects can become reflective about or attain a reflexive relation with regard to themselves, their utterances, and the conditions under which such utterances are made possible and occur. As we have seen, Nietzsche posits that reflectivity comes about when the other is recognised as a threat, an account Butler rejects because the relation to the other is necessarily configured as a form of agonistics. Butler refers to a number of alternative accounts of the relation between recognition, otherness and reflectivity derived from Hegel, and subsequently found in French Marxism, phenomenology, psychoanalytical theory, structuralism and feminism, as well as philosophy. For Hegel:

> the precondition for historical development or dialectical change is provided by the postulate of self-consciousness, a self-identical being, a being confronting another self-consciousness fundamentally the same as itself ... It is only when the object of this self-consciousness turns out to be another self-consciousness that history ... can be said to begin: it is only from the 'moment' there is contradiction and dialectical antagonism that history and thus development and change become possible. (Grosz 1989: 3)

This notion of a productive confrontation between different forms of self-consciousness is formulated by Hegel in the fable of the master and the slave. Two subjects require the other's recognition to serve as a confirmation of their subjectivity, so a struggle ensues between them as to who will recognise the other. This is not a struggle to the death (that would remove the possibility of recognition), but rather to the point where one party values life enough to forsake their autonomy and freedom and submit to the other. They take on the status and roles of master and slave, but given that this is a Hegelian fable, it is the slave who gains most from the arrangement – who becomes, in effect, the actor and agent of history:

> The Master ... is recognized in his human reality and dignity. But this ... is one-sided ... Hence, he is recognized by someone whom he does not – recognize ... this is what is insufficient – what is tragic – in his situation. The Master ... can be satisfied only by recognition from one whom he recognizes as worthy of recognizing him ... But the slave is for him an animal or a thing ... he is not what he wanted to be ... a man recognized by another man ... the satisfied man will necessarily be a Slave, who has passed through Slavery, who has 'dialectically overcome' his slavery ... Consequently, the truth of autonomous Consciousness is slavish Consciousness. (Kojeve 1986: 19–20)

In the Hegelian account, the relation to the outside or the other is productive – it is that which facilitates change, progress, self-awareness and self-transformation. However it is also a process that disorients the subject:

once exposed to the other 'I am invariably transformed by the encounters I undergo; recognition becomes the process by which I become other than what I was and so cease to be able to return to what I was' (Butler 2005: 27). This transformation also precludes any return to the notion of a self-contained, inward-looking subject: 'One is compelled and comported outside oneself ... the only way to know oneself is through a mediation that takes place ... exterior to oneself, by virtue of a convention or a norm one did not make' (p. 28).

It is not clear as to how Hegel's essentially dyadic account of recognition and reflexivity is manifested at the level of socio-cultural practice; in other words, how does an exchange between two subjects 'exceed the perspective of those involved' (p. 28)? The act of recognition both implies and requires a set of conventions, codes and categories through which the other is rendered visible, and which function to facilitate and dispose the praxis that constitute the seeing, reading and evaluating of the world. This is where we can recognise Foucault's 'supplement to Hegel': the understanding that an order of things, a regime of truth 'constrains what will and will not constitute the truth of his self ... the truth by which he might be known and become recognizably human, the account he might give of himself' (p. 30).

Foucault's theories are generally close to Nietzsche's in their emphasis on the cultural politics of meaning and value, the internalisation of imperatives of normalisation, and power being produced through and by agonistic and strategic effects, networks and relations. Both Nietzsche and Foucault insist that the operations and effects of power are productive as well as restrictive. The terror incited by the threat of punishment 'turns out to be strangely fecund' (p. 16), in the sense that enjoyment, cruelty, aggression, sadistic pleasure and violence take so many forms and paths. Foucault, on the other hand, 'refuses to generalize the scene of punishment to account for how a reflexive subject comes about' (p. 15); instead, he posits three conditions or contexts that are productive of, and allow the subject to achieve, some level of desubjugation. First, the distinctions, definitions and differentiations of disciplinary apparatuses and discourses produce categories and subject positions (anti-subjects, non-subjects, delinquent subjects) that are antithetical to the procedures and regimes of normalisation; in other words, the normal and the human are always inhabited by, and constituted from, an excess or remainder, something outside the limits of the subject. Second, the changes to, and the often erratic trajectories of, norms across time and place point to the particularity and arbitrariness of that which claims to be universal – there is always a heterogeneity of historical forms and manifestations of the supposedly homogeneous, timeless and ahistorical. Third and perhaps most importantly, the subject is not simply or necessarily an effect of discourse, but 'forms itself in relation to a set of codes ... and does so in a way that not only ... reveals self-constition to be a kind of poiesis ... but establishes self-making as part of the broader project of critique' (p. 17).

The first two points are reasonably clear and straightforward, but the third, which is central to Foucault's rethinking and refinement of the process of subject formation (Foucault 2001, 2005, 2007), requires further elaboration. Foucault identifies a process or logic whereby what he calls the 'critical attitude' (2007) arises out of the creation, dissemination and deployment of those (historically specific) ideas, imperatives and dispositions that come to constitute or contribute to a particular grid of intelligibility. The example he uses, in an essay/lecture found in *The Politics of Truth* (2007), is that of the emergence, in the fifteenth century and beyond, of a proliferation (Foucault refers to an 'explosion') of discourses, ideas and discussions regarding 'the art of governance':

> There was an explosion in two ways: first, by displacement in relation to the religious centre, let's say if you will, secularisation, the expansion in civil society of this theme of the art of governing men and the method of doing it; and then, second, the proliferation of this art of governing into a variety of areas – how to govern children, how to govern the poor and beggars, how to govern a family, a house ... cities, States and also how to govern one's own body and mind. How to govern was ... a fundamental question which was answered by a multiplication of all the arts of governing – the art of pedagogy, the art of politics, the art of economics, if you will – and of all the institutions of government, in the wider sense the term government had at the time. (2007: 43–4)

Foucault points out, however, that just as the imperative to govern, and the arts and techniques associated with and developed in accordance with it, were colonising socio-cultural fields, there was a response that was highly contrary – what he refers to as extensive questions and considerations about 'how not to be governed' (p. 44). Foucault characterises it as an attitude of distrust and defiance that manifested itself as a determination to find ways and techniques of avoiding or limiting governing. So the preoccupation with the art of governing produced both partners and adversaries; and one particularly significant development along the adversarial plane, taken by Foucault as one possible definition of critique itself, was 'the art of not being governed quite so much' (p. 45).

CRITIQUE

The notion of critique, as Foucault understands it, can be traced back to a specific conjunction of historical circumstances and ideas encompassing the Renaissance, the Reformation, the advent of Humanism, the development of issues and imperatives commensurate and associated with the reason of state, and the rise of the scientific field, along with its culture and set of analytical and epistemological dispositions and techniques.

Foucault argues that disciplinary techniques win out in the end. His work testifies to the efficacy of a set of techniques of observation, regulation, and control that will culminate in our contemporary system of power, which operates without regard to the notion of sovereignty. This other side of the Enlightenment 'inverts revolutionary institutions from within and establishes everywhere the "penitentiary" in place of penal justice' (p. 46). And in texts such as *The Order of Things* (1973), *Discipline and Punish* (1995) and *The Archaeology of Knowledge* (1972), Foucault demonstrates how these procedures feed back into and are eventually articulated within and legitimated by a variety of official, authoritative, scientific discourses (particularly the human sciences).

Foucault's work testifies to 'the importance acquired by scientific and technical rationality in the development of the productive forces and the play of political decisions' (Canguilhem 1991: 12); and yet reflexivity and critique involve and even require attitudes, practices, procedures and methodologies derived from, developed alongside or commensurate with that same scientific and technical rationality. Consider the following extended extract from *The Use of Pleasure*:

> for an action to be 'moral', it must not be reducible to an act or a series of acts conforming to a rule, a law, or a value. Of course all moral action involves a relationship with the reality in which it is carried out, and a relationship with the self. The latter is not simply 'self-awareness' but self-formation as an 'ethical subject', a process in which the individual delimits the part of himself that will

form the object of his moral practice, defines his position relative to the precept he will follow, and decides on a certain mode of being that will serve as his moral goal. And this requires him to act upon himself, to monitor, test, improve, and transform himself. There is no specific moral action that does not refer to a unified moral conduct; no moral conduct that does not call for the forming of oneself as an ethical subject; and no forming of the ethical subject without 'modes of subjectivation' and an 'ascetics' or 'practices of the self' that support them. Moral action is indissociable from the forms of self-activity. (1986: 28)

What is being claimed here? First, the idea of the moral is not reducible to the rule – it is not simply a compliant response to what is already mandatory, whether in the form of a precept ('Do unto others as you would have them do to you'), an injunction ('Thou shalt not commit adultery') or a law ('Guns must be registered'). Second, it involves a process of taking and delimiting oneself as an object of self-formation and ongoing transformation. Third, it requires both thinking through, and an examination, monitoring and testing of, the self in relation to the wider context of the socio-cultural world (and its rules, forms of value, narratives and imperatives). Fourth, this testing of the self takes place via a comparison between a seemingly self-formulated code of conduct (a discourse) and a set or pattern of behaviour (a praxis). As Butler points out, it is significant that whereas many critics have criticised Foucault for undermining the notion of human agency and ethical thought, here he clearly 'turns both to agency and deliberation in new ways in his so-called ethical writings and offers a reformulation of both' (2005: 19).

There are two other points worth making in relation to this claim. First, the process Foucault refers to and describes is intensively technical and methodologically complex: in other words, to some extent the question of agency is subordinate to the question of literacy. Second and relatedly, this kind of intensive and highly literate regime is inexplicable without reference to a set of contexts that make available, authorise, teach, facilitate, reinforce and naturalise what is effectively a reflexive and critical disposition and praxis. If this is a form of agency, it is one made available through and as part of a collective and quite specific habitus; and it requires a more detailed explanation of how 'all moral action involves a relationship with the reality in which it is carried out' (Foucault 1986: 28).

It is in this regard that Bourdieu's work is particularly useful. For Bourdieu, reflexivity is not simply a scholastic or philosophical question abstracted from the world; rather, it is a practical issue, understood as a set of practices and dispositions. It is oriented towards the processes of delimiting tied to our social and cultural origins and categories (generation, class, religion, gender), and our position in whatever field(s) we are located (as anthropologist, journalist, politician). Bourdieu associates a disposition towards reflexivity with a variety of fields and groups, including (but not exclusively) intellectuals (1993: 44), literature and the sciences (Bourdieu and Wacquant 1992: 175), history (Bourdieu and Wacquant 1992: 90) and art (Bourdieu and Haacke 1995: 1). Reflexivity is not, for Bourdieu, associated with one privileged field, but rather is potentially available within any field that disposes its subjects towards 'the systematic exploration of the unthought categories of thought which delimit the thinkable and predetermine the thought' (Bourdieu and Wacquant 1992: 40). Moreover, and as Bourdieu and Wacquant make clear, the taking up of a reflexive attitude should not be understood as the effect of some kind of dramatic Pauline conversion or epiphany; nor is it even, strictly speaking, something that is obtained by the subject-as-agent. Rather, if the field 'is' the subject to a large extent, then any reflexive relation to the doxa of the field must be a constitutive part of that field.

The conditions which bring about, or at least dispose participants in a field towards, reflexivity arise from the very same processes that delimit thought in the first place: subjects in and of a field are shaped, constrained and disposed towards thoughts and actions through their immersion in, and their incorporation of, the procedures, rituals, mechanisms, capital, explicit and implicit rules, and values of the field. In certain fields the rules, procedures and forms of capital are (at least theoretically) oriented towards reflexivity; or, as he would suggest, in those fields it is incumbent upon subjects to think and act in a reflexive manner.

Bourdieu's work on reflexivity provides a relatively grounded explanation – a how and why – of Foucault's account of self-constitution as 'a regime of truth that offers the terms that make self-recognition possible' (Butler 2005: 22). For both Bourdieu and Foucault, the issue of recognition is not a given, but 'is constrained in advance by a regime of truth that decides what will and will not be a recognizable form of being', although 'it does not fully constrain this form' (p. 22). The norms that characterise a particularly discursive regime also constitute the subject who questions; and so to question norms is to bring into jeopardy the truth and sustainability of the self. A subject is recognised and accepted as long as they perform in accordance with the rules, logics, imperatives, values and discourses – the norms – of society. At the same time there are cultural fields where taking a reflexive attitude to the conditions of one's subjectivity is not only something one is disposed towards; it can also constitute a means by which a subject attains capital, and/or it can be recognised as the condition by which the subject lives out and in accordance with the ethos of the field.

To think in a reflexive manner involves, first and foremost, learning to think at and through limits that are themselves constitutive of how we come to see, categorise, understand and relate to the world and to ourselves. Reflexivity, from this perspective, is not quite the same as critique, but it is certainly a close associate. Reflexivity can be seen as that part of critique which, in Foucault's terms, is charged with 'eradicating errors' (2007: 42–3); in other words it has a utility or instrumentality about it.

One of the main issues that Butler addresses in *Giving an Account of Oneself* is how reflexivity or critical thinking constitutes and functions as something other than mere utility, a form of privileged self-indulgence, or basic self-interest – commensurate with and explicable in terms of, at one level or another, Nietzsche's 'bad conscience', Bourdieu's 'misrecognition' or Adorno's 'moral narcissism' (Butler 2005: 112). Foucault claims, for instance, that the instrumental dimension of critique, the 'stiff bit of utility it claims to have', is supplemented or augmented by 'some kind of more general imperative … There is something in critique that is akin to virtue' (Foucault 2007: 42–3). Butler explores this notion of the virtue of critique via a consideration of what is at stake in speaking at and about the level of the limits that demark, constitute and facilitate practices of violence and exclusion. The two accounts she considers are derived from Adorno's work on 'becoming human', and Foucault's theorising of critique and its relation to the concept of parrhesia, or truth telling.

BECOMING HUMAN

For Adorno, the question of the virtue of, or ethical dimension to, the critical attitude is not just about content (identifying what is just, what is human, what is the appropriate response to violence), but also a matter of what we might call the politics and ethics of speech. With regard to the critical distinction between the human and the non-human, for instance, and the violence inherent in such forms of categorisation, Adorno simultaneously asserts the need 'to hold fast to moral norms ... to the question of right and wrong', and cautions against 'the fallibility of the authority' (Butler 2005: 104) that would be in a position to make those assertions. Claiming a right to self-preservation and freedom from the injurious intervention of another always needs to be complemented by a consideration that this 'will to survive' simultaneously opens up the possibility that by 'walling oneself off from injury' (Butler 2005: 103), one is engaging in 'a pure ethics of the self' (p. 113). To reject any association with or responsibility towards human society is, in a sense, to occupy the same ground that enables the human/non-human distinction to be made in the first place. So for Adorno becoming human is always just that – a state that is deferred or in process, rather than an achieved correspondence with, or the negative dimension of, what is prescribed or normalised as human (the abject, the unrecognisable, etc.). As Butler writes, becoming human is:

> no simple task, and it is not always clear when or if one arrives. To be human seems to mean being in a predicament that one cannot solve. In fact, Adorno makes it clear that he cannot define the human for us. If the human is anything, it seems to be a double movement, one in which we assert moral norms at the same time as we question the authority by which we make that assertion. (2005: 103)

The notion of the inhuman constitutes a departure point for critique understood as an ethical practice; more specifically, it is the ground where power and will are manifested at the expense of the other, and where the specific universalises itself.

As such, critique involves speaking against that which makes us behave inhumanly. Speech, here, also means putting oneself on the line, and running the risk of moving, or being categorised, outside of what is normal and recognisable – that is, it involves risking becoming inhuman.

FEARLESS SPEECH

For Butler the issue of what is at stake in, and the limits and conditions of, speech is central to Foucault's later work, particularly in the last two volumes of *The History of Sexuality* (1986, 1988), and the essays, lectures, talks and interviews collected in volumes such as *Fearless Speech* (2001), *The Hermeneutics of the Subject* (2005) and *The Politics of Truth* (2007). Butler writes that for Foucault, in giving an account of oneself:

> one is also exhibiting, in the very speech that one uses, the logos by which one lives. The point is not only to bring speech into accord with action … it is also to acknowledge that speaking is already a kind of doing, a form of action, one that is already a moral practice and a way of life. (Butler 2005: 126)

Foucault devotes the lectures collected in *Fearless Speech* to an analysis and consideration of the Greek concept of parrhesia or 'free speech', which can be dated to the fifth century BC and is still found in use, having evolved in meaning across Greek and Roman culture, eight hundred years later (Foucault 2001: 11).

Parrhesia refers both to a type of content (the parrhesiastes provides a full and candid account of the subject's thoughts and opinions on a particular matter), and a form of relationship (the purpose is not to use rhetorical devices to persuade, but rather to demonstrate to interlocutors that there is a corollary between one's words and one's beliefs and actions). Foucault distinguishes two major forms of parrhesia. One form is perjorative, is often found in anti-democratic and Christian contexts, and refers to a situation where someone speaks without sense or thought. The other form, found most frequently in classical texts, is associated with truthfulness:

> To my mind, the parrhesiastes says what is true because he knows that it is really true. The parrhesiastes is not only sincere and says what is his opinion, but his opinion is also the truth. He says what he knows to be true. The second characteristic of parrhesia, then, is that there is always an exact coincidence between belief and truth. (p. 14)

How can one be sure of 'an exact coincidence' between one's opinion or belief, what one says, and the truth? This question is not just an abstraction: it emerges, more overtly and insistently, in specific cultural fields and across a wider society, when the accounts and discourses that subjects, institutions and communities use to 'speak or show themselves' become the object of analysis; much as when, in Kuhnian terms, a particular paradigm turns its analytical gaze increasingly upon itself (Kuhn 1970). As Butler points out, in asking or posing this question Foucault is focusing attention on one particular historical

context and its vicissitudes with regard to issues of truth telling in order to gain an understanding of both the emergence of the notion of critical thinking and, as a corollary, the contemporary relationship between subjectivity and the operations of power. 'Relinking truth-telling to the problem of power', Foucault:

> remarks that in the fifth century BC philosophical problems emerged in relation to questions about the allocation of power: Who is able to tell the truth, about what, with what consequences, and with what relation to power? Although truth-telling is compelled to proceed according to rules of validity, Foucault also makes clear that there are conditions – I would call them rhetorical – that make truth-telling possible and must be interrogated. In this sense, the problematization of truth must take into account 'the importance of telling the truth, knowing who is able to tell the truth, and knowing why we should tell the truth'. (Butler 2005: 131)

The parrhesiastes is always involved in telling the truth to an audience, whether it is a communal assembly, a friend, or the ruler of a city in order to effect a change of some kind. The audience needs both to comprehend the truth and be moved by it; such a scene is potentially, in Butler's terms, a 'social occasion for self-transformation' (p. 130). Parrhesia constitutes a critical attitude directed at a form of behaviour, irresponsibility, attitude or set of beliefs that stands in the way of the subject's duty; and in making this criticism the parrhesiastes will often point to their own experience and fallibilities – parrhesia can be directed at an other or oneself. The duty that the parrhesiastes is required to perform, first and foremost, is tied to parrhesia itself: it is to facilitate, circulate and demonstrate the truth.

What guarantees parrhesia? What authorises it, testifies to it, demonstrates it? To deal with these questions, we need to return to and reconsider the issue of what is at stake in telling the truth for the parrhesiastes. We had suggested that what was at stake was doing one's duty, but that answer can seem both rhetorical and circular. We can, by way of exemplification, digress here and refer to Slavoj Žižek's analysis of what is, and isn't, at stake in virtual subjectivities played out through Internet chatrooms, games and communities such as *Second Life*:

> The problem of communication in virtual communities is thus not simply that I can lie (that an ... old man can present himself as a ... young woman, etc.) but,

more fundamentally, that I am never truly engaged, since at any moment I can pull back, unhook myself. In virtual community sex games I can be ruthless, I can pour out all my dirty dreams, precisely because my word no longer obliges me, is not 'subjectivized'. (1996: 196)

When Žižek refers to engagement as a precondition of being subjectivised, he is pointing to something that Foucault understands as being constitutive of parrhesia – there are consequences to identifying with or speaking from a subject position (or for that matter and more commonly, being identified by being called the name of a subject category). For Foucault the doubt as to whether one is a parrhesiastes, and what we would call the proof of the authenticity and reliability of the parrhesia, is given in, and guaranteed by, the 'moral qualities' (Foucault 2001: 15) of the speaker. As Foucault writes, the 'parrhesiastic game' presupposes qualities that are 'required to know the truth … and … convey such truth to others' (p. 15).

The reference to parrhesia as a game is deliberate and specific: it refers to the relationship that the parrhesiastes enters into, an exchange played out between interlocutors utilising an agreed set of rules or conventions, and in which something is being played for, or is at stake. One important rule, according to Foucault, is that the parrhesiastes is not only frank, but there is also (and necessarily) 'a risk or danger for him in telling the truth' (p. 16). This is because the parrhesiastes directs a form of criticism while being 'in a position of inferiority with respect to the interlocutor' (p. 18). The position of inferiority is, of course, understood in terms of having access to power of some kind. So when a parrhesiastes rebukes an assembly or majority opinion, there is the risk of a backlash, unpopularity, and in some instances, physical injury or (in the case of Socrates) death. To speak from a position where the interlocutor is in one's power is not an instance of parrhesia, for there is nothing at risk. This returns us to the issue of the moral qualities that characterise the parrhesiastes. Putting oneself in danger because of the necessity of speaking the truth, and the consistency with which one does one's duty despite the possibility of injury or annihilation or alienation (in Classical Athens, unpopular speakers could be and were ostracised), guarantees and embodies the truth that one speaks as the truth of the self:

When you accept the parrhesiastic game in which your own life is exposed, you are taking up a specific relationship to yourself: you risk death to tell the truth instead of reposing in the security of a life where the truth goes unspoken. Of course, the threat of death comes from the Other, and thereby requires a relationship to the Other. But the parrhesiastes primarily chooses a specific relationship to himself: he prefers himself as a truth-teller rather than as a living being who is false to himself. (p. 17).

The questions that Foucault raises and addresses in his description and analysis of parrhesia 'constitute the roots of what we call the "critical tradition", suggesting, perhaps, that we do not regularly include this kind of inquiry as part of the critical tradition, but clearly should' (Butler 2005: 132). Foucault refers to the ways in which parrhesia constitutes the site or locus of various problematics, largely in terms of what we might term their technical aspects (What distinguishes a parrhesiastes or truth teller? How can we 'know' what is authentic parrhesia?), but he also takes into account wider methodological and theoretical issues – 'the problem of truth' (Foucault 2001: 73). Parrhesia-as-problem comes to exemplify and manifest a more general notion of epistemological crisis, transformation or change. As Foucault makes clear, at a local and specific time and place parrhesia initially takes on or is associated with a series of relatively consistent meanings (the parrhesiastes tells all, speaks fearlessly, confronts power) that gradually become problematical; so, for example, as Athenian democracy at the end of the fifth century is corrupted and destabilised by demagoguery, and consequently suffers military reversals and disasters in the Peloponnesian War, this brings into focus the problem 'of recognizing who is capable of speaking the truth within the limits of an institutional system where everyone is entitled to give their opinion' (p. 73).

CONCLUSION

In her recent books Butler has turned her attention, more explicitly, not just to Western 'military reversals and disasters' (for instance, in Iraq and Afghanistan), but also to wider public sphere issues that are associated with those events – the Israeli occupation of Palestine, the discursive violence directed at Muslims, the use of torture in American and other Western military prisons, the racism and xenophobia of post-September 11 America. As we saw in our previous chapter, there is a considerable amount at stake in speaking out on these issues. At best one is ignored or dismissed, by the free media and other institutions of democracy, as naïve and idealist, an unworldly academic; the last adjective is probably redundant here, at least in contemporary media discourses and logics. There are, of course, more serious consequences. To question or criticise the suspension of civil liberties and the use of torture on the part of the United States government can lead to one being labelled anti-patriotic, and a friend and comforter of terrorists. To suggest that the burkha might need to be thought through in terms of what it could mean to the people concerned is a difficult position to take when the doxa, shared by an unlikely coalition of feminists, American right-wing conservatives and the French government, is to treat it as an unambiguous sign of barbarism, to be ridiculed and banned. To speak about, and to call for a criticism of, Israeli policies and practices regarding the Palestinians means, as we saw in the last chapter, being labelled 'anti-Semitic in … effect, if not … intent' (Butler 2006: 101).

What Butler attempts to do, in these and other interventions, is not just to promote empathy or sympathy for victims of violence; rather, she tries to get us to think about and understand the conditions that dispose, and the unthought assumptions that facilitate, those acts of violence. As she writes of the acts of torture and sexual degradation perpetrated in the name of freedom in American military camps in Iraq and elsewhere:

> we can see here the association of a certain cultural presumption of progress with a licence to engage in unbridled destruction … If we ask what kind of freedom this is, it is one that is free of the law at the same time that it is coercive; it is an extension of the logic that establishes state power – and its mechanisms of violence – as beyond the law. (2009: 129)

The term 'freedom' constitutes one of the most significant of the many capitalised ideas that is deployed to organise sense and meaning in the contemporary Western world. It is also, for that reason, one of the most difficult terms to challenge, to engage with, critique, or even to bring to the table of public sphere discussion and analysis. It does its work quickly and without fuss, precisely because any call for consideration and thought with regard to what the terms mean, how it is being used, and for what purposes, is effectively foreclosed. In this way it largely resists critical inquiry.

Butler's oeuvre constitutes a form of critical inquiry. It undertakes what Foucault refers to, in contradistinction to the doxa of the field of power, as 'the undefined work of freedom' (1997: 316). Critical inquiry is directed at the limitations of thought that are in fact constitutive of thought – with the aim of producing freedom from the 'limits of ourselves' (p. 316). This is not a universal and universalising project akin to Marxism or other post-Hegelian versions of the Enlightenment project. The space opened up by critical inquiry must always 'put itself to the test of ... contemporary reality, both to grasp the points where change is possible and desirable, and to determine the precise form this change should take' (p. 316).

For Foucault, critical inquiry is informed by this specific sensibility and ethos. Butler's work is predicated on and constituted from this ethos, performing as it does a necessary and consistent correlation between a subject's values, accounts and practices. In these and other issues she has increasingly taken on the role that can perhaps be best characterised by way of reference to the function and responsibility of the parrhesiastes – to tell all, speak fearlessly, and to confront power.

FURTHER READING

Foucault, M. (1997) *Ethics*. London: Penguin.
Foucault, M. (2001) *Fearless Speech*. Los Angeles: Semiotext(e).
Foucault, M. (2007) *The Politics of Truth*. Los Angeles: Semiotext(e).

Glossary

Anaclisis: Freudian notion whereby the initial instinct of self-preservation (sucking the breast for nourishment) is used as a kind of prop by the sexual instincts.

Bio-power: for Foucault, the process by which power and knowledge works to dispose and regulate bodies.

Bodily hexis: the forms of bodies, and bodily movements and deportment, that are commensurate with, authorised by, and appropriately reflect the values of, a cultural field.

Butch-femme: a type of lesbian relationship in which one partner identifies with nominally masculine traits (the butch), and the other partner identifies with nominally feminine traits (the femme). Butch-femme has a specific social and political history, and is not reducible to an imitation of heterosexuality.

Camp: sensibility or gender performance characterised by artifice, irony and stylisation, and often associated with gay men.

Constructivism, constructionism: the notion that social or bodily traits often represented as natural are in fact socially and culturally produced. Usually positioned as the opposite of essentialism.

Critique, critical inquiry: a space opened up by the testing of reality in order to evaluate the possibility and desirability of change, and determine the forms it will take.

Cultural field: is a concept taken from Bourdieu; it can be defined as a set of institutions, rules, categories, discourses, dispositions, forms of capital and practices which form an objective hierarchy, and which produce and authorise identities.

Desire: for Hegel desire is understood as, or stands in for, reflexive consciousness, whereby consciousness seeks to know and comprehend itself through the mediation of otherness. Psychoanalysis posits desire as something that is sent away or repressed in order that the subject can exist; however repressed desire always returns without overtly manifesting or articulating itself, for instance in dreams. Desire for Nietzsche and Deleuze is the will manifested as the affirmation of life-as-force. For Foucault desire is, first and foremost, a name with a history; in other words, its status is fundamentally discursive.

Discourse: a kind of language that is specific to, and authorised by, cultural fields, and which categorises the world.

Essentialism: the idea that there is a necessary connection between the body and certain dispositions and forms of behaviour.

Ethics: understood as a necessary and consistent correlation between a subject's values, accounts and practices.

Foreclosure: the process whereby a subject's bodily dispositions and forms of identification are constrained as a consequence of non-normative alternatives being rendered unthinkable.

Gender: a set of bodily characteristics, values, desires, orientations, practices and typologies that are tied, through the operations of power, to the categories of male and female. According to Butler, feminist theory has tended to position gender as something one has, whereas she argues gender is something one does.

Genealogy: the attempt to trace and locate the moments and sites when power produces and naturalises meaning or sense.

Habitus: a set of dispositions, values and ways of seeing derived from our cultural trajectories, and which generate practices. Bourdieu characterises it as 'history naturalised'.

Heteronormativity: the naturalisation of heterosexual desire as the norm. Butler argues that this also naturalises gender categories.

Hyperbolic mimicry: the citation and reproduction of an authorised gender performance as exaggeration or excess.

Identity: the subject takes on an identity within processes of discursive designation and location: the body-as-content is designated as being commensurate, or otherwise, with regard to socio-cultural and/or scientific categories, and is thus inscribed in terms of certain meanings, values, dispositions, orientations and narratives.

Incest taboo: the social prohibition that forbids sexual relations between close relatives.

Interpellation: refers to the process whereby power calls, addresses and categorises subjects.

Melancholia: is conventionally characterised in psychoanalysis as nonfunctional grieving. The melancholic subject psychically refuses to acknowledge the loss of the love-object, and may withdraw from the world, responsibilities, and regard for the self or others.

Mourning: is characterised as a relatively functional and non-pathological response to a loss.

Normalisation, norms: the association of bodily exemplars and typologies with authorised meanings, narratives and values in order to discipline, dispose and orient subjects.

Parrhesia: the Greek concept of parrhesia or 'free speech' can be dated to the fifth century BC. It refers both to a type of content (the parrhesiastes provides a full and candid account of the subject's thoughts and opinions on a particular matter), and a form of relationship (the purpose is not to use rhetorical devices to persuade, but rather to demonstrate to interlocutors that there is a corollary between one's words and one's beliefs and actions).

Performativity: linguistic performativity refers to speech acts that effect what they announce ('I dare you'; 'I sentence you'). Butler adapts this into a theory of gender performativity whereby certain announcements or performances of gender produce the effects they seem to describe (the announcement 'It's a girl' inaugurates the process of girling). Central to the theory of gender performativity are the mechanisms of citation and repetition.

Queer: in queer theory, queer usually refers to the use and performance of categories of sex, gender and sexuality in ways that disturb their taken-for-granted meanings. Queer performances are not outside those categories of identity; they use frameworks of identity against themselves in order to expose their contradictions, and the operations of power that sustain those categories.

Reflexivity: to think at, and through, limits that are constitutive of how we come to see, categorise, understand and relate to the world and to ourselves.

Sex: the two primary discursive categories (male and female) that render a body recognisable as a subject.

Sex/gender distinction: an influential framework in feminist theory that posits sex as the natural/biological differences between men and women, and gender as the cultural meanings attached to those differences. Butler critiques this distinction, and argues that both sex and gender are discursively produced.

Sexuality: libidinal regimes, orientations, dispositions and practices. In Western culture these are often understood as constituting an identity (so a man's sexual desire for another man constitutes him as a homosexual), an understanding that Foucault argues is a product of particular discursive regimes.

Subject: the result of a process involving the reiteration of discourses, performances and narratives of, and the repeated confirmation of relations of value regarding, the body, that make that body potentially visible and recognisable as a coherent set of forms, categories and meanings.

Subjection: Butler refers to the situation where the subject is not only constituted through and dominated by, but also remains necessarily tied to and reliant on, the practices and discourses of power, as a form of subjection.

Symbolic violence: the techniques, discourses and regimes of practice whereby the other is dehumanised or rendered abject.

Transgender: often used as an umbrella term that includes any body, gender performance, or gender identification that is at odds with, or deliberately critiques, the binary understanding of sex as either male or female. This may include (but is not limited to): transsexuals, drag queens and kings, transvestites, tomboys, butches and femmes, intersex people, and cross-dressers.

Bibliography

Abelove, H. et al. (eds) (1993) *The Lesbian and Gay Studies Reader*. New York: Routledge.

Adams, W. (2009) 'Could This Women's World Champ Be a Man?', *TIME*, 21 August. Last accessed 16 March 2010, available at http://www.time.com/time/world/article/0,8599,1917767,00.html#ixzz0iJ9srV5A

Althusser, L. (1977) *Lenin and Philosophy and Other Essays*. London: New Left Books.

Altman, D. (1972) *Homosexuals: Oppression and Liberation*. Sydney: Angus and Robertson.

Appadurai, A. (1997) *Modernity at Large*. Minneapolis: University of Minnesota Press.

Austin, J.L. (1962) *How To Do Things With Words*. Oxford: Oxford University Press.

Austin, J.L. (1970) *Philosophical Papers* (J. Urmson & G. Warnock (eds)). Oxford: Oxford University Press.

Beauvoir, S. (1973) *The Second Sex* (trans. E. Parshley). New York: Vintage Books.

Benhabib, S. et al. (1995) *Feminist Contentions*. New York: Routledge.

Best, S. & Kellner, D. (1991) *Postmodern Theory*. London: Macmillan.

Bourdieu, P. (1990) *Outline of a Theory of Practice* (trans. R. Nice). Cambridge: Cambridge University Press.

Bourdieu P. (1993) *The Field of Cultural Production*. Cambridge: Polity Press.

Bourdieu, P. (1998a) *On Television and Journalism*. London: Pluto Press.

Bourdieu, P. (1998b) *The State Nobility*. Cambridge: Polity Press.

Bourdieu, P. (2000) *Pascalian Meditations* (trans. R. Nice). Cambridge: Polity Press.

Bourdieu, P. (2001) *Masculine Domination*. Cambridge: Polity Press.

Bourdieu, P. (2004) *Science of Science and Reflexivity* (trans. R. Nice). Cambridge: Polity Press.

Bourdieu, P. & Haacke, H. (1995) *Free Exchange*. Cambridge: Polity Press.

Bourdieu, P. & Wacquant, L. (1992) *An Invitation to Reflexive Sociology*. Chicago: University of Chicago Press.

Bradshaw, P. (2009) 'Bruno', *guardian.co.uk*, 10 July. Last accessed 16 March 2010, available at http://www.guardian.co.uk/film/2009/jul/10/film-review-bruno

Burchill, G. et al. (1991) *The Foucault Effect*. Chicago: University of Chicago Press.

Butler, J. (1987) *Subjects of Desire*. New York: Columbia University Press.

Butler, J. (1990) *Gender Trouble*. New York: Routledge.

Butler, J. (1991) 'Imitation and Gender Insubordination', *Inside/Out: Lesbian Theories, Gay Theories*. New York: Routledge.

Butler, J. (1993) *Bodies That Matter*. New York: Routledge.

Butler, J. (1997a) *Excitable Speech*. New York: Routledge.

Butler, J. (1997b) *The Psychic Life of Power*. Stanford: Stanford University Press.

Butler, J. (1997c) 'Merely Cultural', *Social Texts*, 15 (3/4).

Butler, J. (1997d) 'Against Proper Objects', in E. Weed & N. Schor (eds), *Feminism Meets Queer Theory*. Bloomington: Indiana University Press.

Butler, J. (1999) *Gender Trouble* (Anniversary Edition). New York: Routledge.

Butler, J. (2000) *Antigone's Claim*. New York: Columbia University Press.

Butler, J. (2004) *Undoing Gender*. New York: Routledge.

Butler, J. (2005) *Giving an Account of Oneself*. New York: Fordham University Press.

Butler, J. (2006) *Precarious Life*. London: Verso.

Butler, J. (2009) *Frames of War*. London: Verso.

Butler, J. & Martin, B. (1994) 'Cross-Identifications', *Diacritics*, 24 (2/3).

Butler, J. & Spivak, G. (2007) *Who Sings the Nation State?* London: Seagull Books.

Butler, J. et al. (2000) *Contingency, Hegemony, Universality*. London: Verso.

Canguilhem, G. (1991) *The Normal and the Pathelogical* (trans. C. Fawcett). New York: Zone Books.

Cavarero, A. (2000) *Relating Narratives* (trans. P. Kottman). London: Routledge.

Certeau, M. (1988) *The Practice of Everyday Life*. Berkeley: University of California Press.

de Lauretis, T. (1991) '"Queer Theory": Lesbian and Gay Sexualities', *Differences: A Journal of Feminist Cultural Studies* 3 (2).

Deleuze, G. and Guattari, F. (1989) *Anti-Oedipus* (trans. R. Hurley et al.). Minneapolis: University of Minnesota Press.

Derrida, J. (1976) *On Grammatology*. Baltimore: Johns Hopkins University Press.

Derrida, J. (1982) *Margins of Philosophy* (trans. A. Bass). Chicago: University of Chicago Press.

Derrida, J. (1988) *Limited Inc.* Evanston: Northwestern University Press.

Dhaliwal, N. (2009) 'Bruno is a Product of Sacha Baron Cohen's Bourgeois Sexual Neuroses', *guardian.co.uk*, 9 July. Last accessed 16 March 2010, available at http://www.guardian.co.uk/film/filmblog/2009/jul/09/bruno-sacha-baron-cohen

Dyer, R. (2002) *The Matter of Images*. London: Routledge.

Epstein, D. (2009) 'Biggest Issue Surrounding Semenya Remains Unanswered', *SI.com*, 19 November. Last accessed 16 March 2010, available at http://sportsillustrated. cnn.com/2009/writers/david_epstein/11/19/caster.semenya/index.html

Everett, C. (2009) 'Adam Lambert Delivers Raunchy AMA Performance Filled with Hip Thrusts, Crotch Grabs and a Makeout', *New York Daily News*, 23 November. Last accessed 1 March 2010, available at http://www.dailynews.com/gossip,2009/11/23/

2009-11-23_adam_lambert_delivers_raunchy_ama_performance_filled_with_hip_thrusts_crotch_gr.html

Foucault, M. (1972) *The Archaeology of Knowledge* (trans. A. Sheridan Smith). New York: Tavistock.

Foucault, M. (1973) *The Order of Things*. New York: Vintage Books.

Foucault, M. (ed.) (1980a) *Herculine Barbin* (trans. R. McDougall). New York: Colophon.

Foucault, M. (1980b) *Power/Knowledge* (trans. C. Gordon et al.). New York: Pantheon Books.

Foucault, M. (1986) *The Use of Pleasure* (trans. R. Hurley). New York: Vintage Books.

Foucault, M. (1988) *The Care of the Self* (trans. R. Hurley). New York: Vintage Books.

Foucault, M. (1991) *The Foucault Reader* (P. Rabinow (ed.)). London: Penguin.

Foucault, M. (1995) *Discipline and Punish* (trans. A. Sheridan). New York: Vintage Books.

Foucault, M. (1997) *Ethics* (P. Rabinow (ed.)). London: Penguin.

Foucault, M. (2001) *Fearless Speech*. Los Angeles: Semiotext(e).

Foucault, M. (2005) *The Hermeneutics of the Subject* (trans. G. Burchell). New York: Picador.

Foucault, M. (2007) *The Politics of Truth* (trans. L. Hochroth & C. Porter). Los Angeles: Semiotext(e).

Foucault, M. (2008) *The History of Sexuality* (trans. R. Hurley). London: Penguin.

Freud, S. (1984) *On Metapsychology* (trans. A. Richards). Harmondsworth: Penguin.

Freud, S. (1987) *Case Histories 11* (trans. A. Richards). Harmondsworth: Penguin.

Fuss, D. (1989) *Essentially Speaking*. New York: Routledge.

Fuss, D. (ed.) (1991) *Inside/Out*. New York: Routledge.

Grosz, E. (1989) *Sexual Subversions*. Sydney: Allen and Unwin.

Grosz, E. (1990) *Jacques Lacan*. Sydney: Allen and Unwin.

Grosz, E. (1995) *Space, Time and Perversion*. Sydney: Allen and Unwin.

Guardian (2009) 'Caster Semenya Found "Innocent of Any Wrong" to Retain 800m Gold Medal', *guardian.co.uk*, 19 November. Last accessed 16 March 2010, available at http://www.guardian.co.uk/sport/2009/nov/19/caster-semenya-athletics-south-africa

Hall, D. (2003) *Queer Theories*. Basingstoke: Palgrave.

Halperin, D. (1995) *Saint Foucault*. New York: Oxford University Press.

Hennessy, R. (2000) *Profit and Pleasure*. New York: Routledge.

Jagger, G. (2008) *Judith Butler*. London: Routledge.

Jagose, A. (1996) *Queer Theory*. Dunedin: Otago University Press.

Jeffrey, S. (1989) 'Butch and Femme: Now and Then', *Not a Passing Phase*, Lesbian History Group (eds). London: Women's Press.

Jeffreys, S. (1996) 'Queerly Unconstrained', *Meanjin, 55* (1).

Jeffreys, S. (2003) *Unpacking Queer Politics*. Cambridge: Polity Press.

Kafka, F. (1961) *Metamorphosis and Other Stories* (trans. M. Secker). Harmondsworth: Penguin.

Kafka, F. (1976) *The Trial* (trans. W. Muir & E. Muir). Harmondsworth: Penguin.

Kanner, M. (2004) 'Questions for Queer Eyes', *Gay and Lesbian Review Worldwide*, 11 (2).

Keller, E. F. (1985) *Reflections on Gender and Science*. New Haven: Yale University Press.

Kirsch, M. (2000) *Queer Theory and Social Change*. London: Routledge.

Kojeve, A. (1986) *Introduction to the Reading of Hegel* (trans. J. Nichols). Ithaca: Cornell University Press.

Kotz, L. (1992) 'The Body You Want', *Art Forum International*, 81 (1).

Kuhn, T. (1970) *The Structure of Scientific Revolutions*. Chicago: University of Chicago Press.

Lacan, J. (1977) *Ecrits: A Selection* (trans. A. Sheridan). New York: Norton.

Laplanche, J. (1990) *Life and Death in Psychoanalysis*. Baltimore: Johns Hopkins University Press.

Laplanche, J. & Pontalis, J. (1988) *The Language of Psychoanalysis* (trans. D. Nicholson-Smith). London: Karnac Books.

Lefort, C. (1986) *The Political Forms of Modern Society*. Cambridge, MA: MIT Press.

Lloyd, M. (2008) *Judith Butler*. Cambridge: Polity Press.

Lyttle, J. (2004) 'Wake Up, Britain: We Gays Have Moved On', *New Statesman*, 30 August.

Martin, B. (1994) 'Sexualities without Gender and Other Queer Utopias', *Diacritics*, 24 (2–3).

Meyer, M. (ed.) (1994) *The Politics and Poetics of Camp*. London: Routledge.

Morton, D. (1995) 'Birth of the Cyberqueer', *PMLA*, 110 (3).

Nietzsche, F. (1956) *The Birth of Tragedy and The Genealogy of Morals* (trans. F. Golffing). New York: Doubleday Anchor.

Nussbaum, M. C. (1999) 'The Professor of Parody: The Hip Defeatism of Judith Butler', *The New Republic*, 22 February.

Prosser, J. (2006) 'Judith Butler: Queer Feminism, Transgender, and the Transubstantiation of Sex', in S. Stryker & S. Whittle (eds), *The Transgender Studies Reader*. New York: Routledge.

Reiter, R. (ed.) (1975) *Towards an Anthropology of Women*. New York: Monthly Review Press.

Rubin, G. (1975) 'The Traffic in Women', *Towards an Anthropology of Women* (R. Reiter (ed.)). New York: Monthly Review Press.

Rubin, G. (1984) 'Thinking Sex: Notes for a Radical Theory of the Politics of Sexuality', in C. Vance (ed.), *Pleasure and Danger*. London: Routledge.

Sedgwick, E. (1990) *Epistemology of the Closet*. Berkeley: University of California Press.

Sedgwick, E. (1993) *Tendencies*. Durham, NC: Duke University Press.

Sullivan, N. (2003) *A Critical Introduction to Queer Theory*. New York: New York University Press.

Turner, W. (2000) *A Genealogy of Queer Theory*. Philadelphia: Temple University Press.

Vanasco, J. (2009) 'How Adam Lambert is Hurting Gay Marriage', *The Huffington Post*, 24 November. Last accessed 18 March, available at http://www.huffingtonpost.com/jennifer-vanasco/why-adam-lambert-is-right_b_369274.html

Vance, C. (ed.) (1984) *Pleasure and Danger*. New York: Routledge.

Warner, M. (ed.) (1993) *Fear of a Queer Planet*. Minneapolis: Minnesota University Press.

Warner, M. (1999) *The Trouble with Normal*. New York: The Free Press.

Weed, E. (1997) 'Introduction', *Feminism Meets Queer Theory*. Bloomington: Indiana University Press.

Weed, E. & Schor, N. (eds) (1997) *Feminism Meets Queer Theory*. Bloomington: Indiana University Press.

Weedon, C. (1987) *Feminist Practice and Poststructuralist Theory*. Oxford: Blackwell.

Weeks, J. (1985) *Sexuality and its Discontents*. London: Routledge.

Williams, C. (1997) 'Feminism and Queer Theory: Allies or Antagonists', *Australian Feminist Studies*, 12 (26).

Wittig, M. (1980) 'The Straight Mind', *Feminist Issues* 1 (1) Summer.

Wittig, M. (1983) 'The Point of View: Universal or Particular', *Feminist Issues* 3 (2) Fall.

Žižek, S. (1996) *The Indivisible Remainder*. London: Verso.

Žižek, S. (1997) 'Multiculturalism, or the Cultural Logic of Multinational Capitalism', *New Left Review*, 225.

Index